GOD AT THE EDGE

Also by Niles Elliot Goldstein

Spiritual Manifestos:
Visions for Renewed Religious Life in America from Young Spiritual Leaders of Many Faiths
(editor)

Duties of the Soul:
The Role of Commandments in Liberal Judaism
(edited with Peter S. Knobel)

Forests of the Night:
The Fear of God in Early Hasidic Thought

Judaism and Spiritual Ethics
(with Steven S. Mason)

GOD AT THE EDGE

searching for the divine in uncomfortable and unexpected places

niles elliot goldstein

BELL TOWER NEW YORK

Grateful acknowledgment is made to the following for permission to reprint previously published material: *New Directions Publishing Corporation:* Excerpts from *The Wisdom of the Desert* by Thomas Merton. Copyright © 1960 by the Abbey of Gethsemani, Inc. Reprinted by permission of New Directions Publishing Corporation. *The University of Chicago Press:* Select passages from St. John of the Cross, *The Poems of St. John of the Cross,* translated by John Frederick Nims. Reprinted by permission of the University of Chicago Press.

Portions of this book have previously appeared in *Newsweek, Moment, Blue,* and *The Forward,* and brief passages in two of my earlier books, *Duties of the Soul* and *Spiritual Manifestos.*

Published by Bell Tower, New York, New York.
Member of the Crown Publishing Group.

Random House, Inc. New York, Toronto, London, Sydney, Auckland
www.randomhouse.com

Printed in the United States of America

Design by Barbara Balch

Library of Congress Cataloging-in-Publication Data
Goldstein, Niles Elliot, 1966–
God at the edge : searching for the divine in uncomfortable and unexpected places / Niles Elliot Goldstein.—1st ed.
p. cm.
Includes bibliographical references.
1. Goldstein, Niles Elliot, 1966– 2. Rabbis—New York (State)—New York—Biography. 3. Spiritual life—Judaism. 4. Spiritual life—Christianity. 5. Suffering—Religious aspects—Judaism. I. Title.

BM755.G64 A3 2000
296.7—dc21 99-047236

ISBN 0-609-60499-6

10 9 8 7 6 5 4 3 2 1

First Edition

For all my teachers,

those whom I met at the edge

and those who pushed me there

contents

acknowledgments

This book is the result of a decade of powerful and sometimes difficult experiences, and of at least three years of trying to make sense of them all in the context of my life as a man and a rabbi. It is also due in no small measure to the attention and efforts of people other than myself. Bonny Fetterman, my friend, former editor, and literary guru, helped me with the early manuscript in a number of ways, particularly in finding the right home for it. I will always be grateful for her guidance and assistance. My agent, Ellen Geiger, has shared with me her experience and wisdom and aided me in more fully understanding the mysterious world of book publishing. She is a great advocate, and I am glad she is on my side.

Several of my friends served as readers for this book and offered me opinions and advice that were very insightful and extremely helpful. Back in 1996, when I started working on the book, Ina Aronow and Cullen Stanley were direct in their feedback and encouraging in their support. Since then, Elizabeth Barrett, Dan Bronstein, Lynne Bundesen, Philip Friedman, Madeline Goff, and Jenny Lorant have read and assisted me with various parts of the book. I appreciate their help and, more important, treasure our relationships. Patricia Gift, who has been a reader and a friend throughout this process, has also become something of a counselor and confidante. I value her friendship. I also thank Debbie Koenig and Katherine Beitner for their energy and support.

I want to thank most of all my editor at Bell Tower, Toinette Lippe. I could not have asked for anyone better or easier to work with on a book—especially this one. None of her commitment, attentiveness, reliability, patience, or enthusiasm went unnoticed. With individuals such as Toinette in a publishing industry that is becoming ever more commercial and uninspiring, there is still hope that good books will see the light of day.

Finally, I am grateful to God, who is ultimately behind all things—whether pleasant or challenging. I view becoming a rabbi as my way of expressing that gratitude, and with deep humility I offer this book as part of my devotion. May it serve as an aid to others in their search for spiritual meaning and fulfillment.

introduction

Much of what passes for spirituality these days is approached from a perspective that is comforting and clean. There are twelve steps for this, seven rules for that, and guardian angels to help us with all of our problems along the way. A great many books on the topic, as well as the motivational speakers who go with them, seem to focus exclusively on the brighter side of spiritual issues, on getting in touch with the serenity, sensitivity, and self-love that are often beyond our grasp. Sometimes these books and individuals go out of their way to accentuate the happier aspects of life, offering uplifting messages of boundless optimism and hope.

While such messages are important and speak to many people, they do not resonate with all of us, nor do they deal adequately with the experiences of struggle and pain. Reality can be messy, and it can frequently force us to reduce our expectations and rein in our hopes. Not everyone can find spiritual fulfillment in a place that feels inviting and safe, like a self-help book or a house of worship. There is a long history of people discovering God in unexpected, unusual, sometimes even uncomfortable contexts. It can occur in a place of darkness, at the *edge*. Judaism was born in the wilderness of the desert, at the foot of a mountain, as a people cringed in terror. Christianity traces its origins to a man dying on a cross, crying out in doubt and despair.

While American popular culture has generally approached spirituality from a lighter perspective, the world around us has fallen prey to decidedly darker forces. A thousand years ago panic swept over Europe as people thought that the end of history was at hand. Monks stopped copying manuscripts, and construction on new religious buildings came to a halt. Today, as we step into the next millennium, similar apocalyptic impulses have surfaced. We have doomsday cults, survivalist groups, and religious fanaticism. We fear nuclear catastrophe, AIDS, overpopulation, global warming, even alien invasion.

Nietzsche warns us, "If you gaze long into an abyss, the abyss will gaze back into you." But there can be darkness without doom. The edge does not have to lead to nihilism. If we are careful, it is possible to recognize, accept, even *grow* from spirituality's borderlands without being consumed by them. As a seminarian and now as a young rabbi, I have never been drawn to the religious center, but I am not alone. I am just one link in a very long chain of spiritual malcontents, a chain that extends into our own time. Historically, when the mainstream has been stunted, many have looked to the fringes for their spiritual life.

We have alternative medicine and alternative music. Why not alternative religious expression? In an age when religion has been deconstructed and decentralized, I have started to construct the religious life and lifestyle that I know I will need in order to heed my particular calling: a rabbinate on the edge. In a way, the reshaping of religion in America has opened up new doors for the clergy. Our career paths are no longer spelled out for us in advance. We can work in a variety of noncongregational settings and hold a range of professional positions that those who came before us could never have thought possible. There are hospital pastors, campus ministers, television preachers, and a host of other career options. None of them have appealed to me. So I have tried to go a step further. I have tried to take my faith to the frontier.

In the past, men and women found God—and their particular spiritual expressions—in bushes that burned, valleys of shadows, and dens of lions. Some communed with the divine on the peaks of mountains. Others had mystical encounters in prison cells. Itinerant rabbis and explorer priests followed their callings to remote shtetls and uncharted villages. Some found the fullest manifestation of their faith through solitude, hunger, or other forms of denial. Some even found it through death and martyrdom. I understand the impulse toward the edge. My own experience with spirituality has taken place not only in synagogues and through holy books, but in dogsleds, squad cars, and cyberspace. It has taken me to the tundra of Alaska and the steppes of Central Asia. Existential struggle, not equanimity, has been the impetus for my quest, a quest that has uncovered the divine image within me but also brought me face-to-face with my inner darkness and demons.

Authentic works on spirituality have never been afraid to journey to the frontiers of personal experience. Avoiding the darker dimension of the human soul (and its interactions with the world of the spirit) will lead only to scratching the outer crust of our inner worlds. We may feel good as a result. We may think we have found all the answers. But with this approach we will never shake off our false sense of security or encounter the full spectrum of spiritual experiences. This book is about, and for, all those who have struggled to find God in the religious mainstream and have had to look elsewhere. Kierkegaard calls God the Absolute Frontier. It sometimes *does* take a journey to the edge, into territory that is not always comfortable, to discover the spiritual sustenance we so often crave. The dark forest of the inner spirit may be murky in places, but buried in its soil are the seeds of our salvation.

Then Moses caused Israel to set out from the Sea of Reeds. They went on into the wilderness of Shur; they traveled three days in the wilderness and found no water. They came to Marah, but they could not drink the water of Marah because it was bitter; that is why it was named Marah. And the people grumbled against Moses, saying, "What shall we drink?" So he cried out to the Lord, and the Lord showed him a piece of wood; he threw it into the water and the water became sweet.

EXODUS 15:22–25

GOD AT THE EDGE

1 / under lock and key

I wanted to be left alone in my mousehole. The whiff of real life had overwhelmed me, and I couldn't breathe.

FYODOR DOSTOYEVSKY, *Notes from Underground*

The cop behind the camera hung a row of numbers around my neck and snapped two pictures: one as I faced him and one after I turned to the side. Another officer took off my handcuffs and ordered me to remove my shoelaces. I leaned forward and placed them on the desk in front of me. "Now your belt," he said. I slid the leather strap through the loops of my jeans, rolled it into a coil, and set it next to the laces. "Got a comb?" he asked. I nodded, and he gestured for me to put it with the other items. The first cop, an older, miserable-looking man with the knot of his necktie pulled down to his sternum, demanded my wallet, extracted the cash from it, and handed it back to me. He then stuffed everything on the desk into a large yellow envelope, sealed it, and wrote my name and number on the front. After filling out a form, he turned it toward me and gave me his pen. "Sign it," he said. The line at the top of the page read CENTRAL BOOKING: PROPERTY FORM. But it was the line at the bottom that jarred my soul: SIGNATURE: PRISONER.

Just a few hours before, I had been with a friend at a trendy nightclub in midtown Manhattan. I felt good. A beautiful woman I'd been eyeing all night was buying me drinks at the bar. I was going to graduate from college in just over a week. On the surface, all seemed right with the world. I was strong. Free. Buzzing on life in a pleasure dome of youth. The Johnnie Walker was kicking in. I excused myself from the woman to go to the rest room. As I descended the stairs toward the toilets, though, an overwhelming sense of doom came over me. At the same time, something started to erupt from within me. Rage. I passed the washroom attendant. He greeted me, but I walked past him in silence. Soon I stood face-to-face with a brick wall. Blood roiled in my veins. Like an unrelenting wound, a single thought throbbed inside my skull: *We're all going to die.*

I had open heart surgery when I was three years old. Although I never had any physical effects from the experience (other than an enormous scar that curled around my left side), it affected me psychically, made me unable to live fully in the present. My satisfactions and joys had always been stunted by a crushing awareness of human mortality, a feeling in my guts that anything good, anything at *all*, would eventually come to an end. Now it was happening again. But after two decades of trying to suppress my despair and frustration, after struggling to sublimate my darker impulses through wrestling, rugby, and carousing, everything boiled over in a senseless act of destruction. I ripped the urinal out of the wall, and it shattered at my feet. Suddenly the attendant appeared. He stared at the broken marble fixture, and with one word—"Asshole!"—he raced upstairs. I knew he was getting the bouncers, but I didn't really care. Whatever was going to happen next was out of my control. My spasm of violence felt almost liberating. I washed my hands and climbed the steps back toward the club. There was a back door at the top of the stairs that led out to the street. I paused in front of it. For an instant I considered running, but I didn't. And before I could turn around again, several muscular arms grabbed me from behind. I was surrounded by a group of bouncers. I wasn't going anywhere.

The police arrived a few minutes later. After the attendant explained to them what I'd done, they told me to turn around and face the wall. I was put in handcuffs, led out of the nightclub (and away from my friend and the woman), and placed in a squad car. I was charged with criminal mischief. The alcohol helped to numb my fear, but I knew I was about to experience something that was not going to be pleasant. At the precinct house, I was led down a narrow corridor and put into a small holding pen. A cop removed the cuff from my right wrist, pushed me onto the bench, and then fastened it again around one of the bars. There was one other occupant in the pen already, a wiry teenager. He looked terrified. The officer who was typing up his paperwork spoke to him.

"You're in big trouble, man," he said. "You might've really killed somebody tonight, Joe. Think about it. Tonight you might have actually killed a man."

The teenager, who was staring at the floor, started crying. "I didn't do nothin'," he said.

"But we've got witnesses that saw you drop the gun, Joe," the officer said. "Tell me more about the gun." The two of them seemed to know each other. It was almost like watching a father trying to teach his child a lesson about telling the truth.

"I told you," he cried, "I didn't do nothin'."

I was chained to the same cell as someone who might be a murderer. The whiskey was beginning to wear off, and I was growing more and more anxious. *What am I doing here?* It was my inability to cope with human limitations—my refusal to accept life on its own terms—that had driven me to this place. My anger had forced me into even narrower confines. The officer who was working on my forms told me that I could make a phone call if I wanted to. Who was I going to call? My parents? They were back in Chicago. And what would I say to them: "Mom, Dad, I've been arrested because I'm afraid of dying"? I declined to call anybody. After half an hour or so the officer removed me from the pen and proceeded to take my fingerprints. With my hands firmly in his, moving as if he'd rehearsed these motions hundreds of times, he left black imprints of each of my fingertips and thumbs in ten little boxes on a cardboard sheet. I asked him if I could wash my hands in a sink a few feet away. "What do you think this is," he said, "a Holiday Inn? Dry them on your pants. This is *jail*, man. You're in jail."

He led me through the precinct house back to the street, where the other officer who had picked me up was waiting behind the wheel of the squad car. We drove off. I didn't know New York well, and I had no idea where we were headed. The two of them made small talk in the front seat and ignored me. It was three or four in the morning. I gazed out of the window at the vacant streets and empty shops. Manhattan looked eerie, surreal. But this was no dream. I was on a dark journey into a world I'd never seen before. We pulled into a driveway with a barbed-wire gate and stopped. A guard opened it and waved us through. The gate closed behind us. We stopped again in front of a back door to a huge building. The officers took me out of the car and handed me over, like a baton, to a new officer, who escorted me toward the door. Without a word, without even looking at me, the cops who'd arrested me got back into the car and left the compound.

That was how I arrived at Central Booking. And that was just the beginning of what the cops referred to as "the System." After I signed the prisoner's property form, I was led to a different area of the large, central room where they had photographed me. Still in handcuffs, I was met by a gigantic bald man. Sticking out of his hip pocket were two rubber gloves. "Don't move," someone said. The man frisked me, pulling out all my pockets and feeling up and down my legs and arms. When he started to unzip my fly I broke into a sweat. *What do they think I am?* The bald man slid my jeans down to my knees and told me to bend over. Looking between my legs, I saw him slide on the rubber gloves. Someone handed him a flashlight. He reached forward and painfully separated my buttocks, shining the light inside and groping around with his fingers. I felt like a dog.

When it was over, I was led to another room, an immense holding pen much bigger than the one from the precinct house. The numbness that had replaced my rage was now itself replaced by fear. A man was lying down just on the other side of the bars, and when he saw me come forward he said, "This is my house." The cop unlocked the door and pushed me in, slamming it shut behind me. I had to step over the man on the floor, who kept on muttering, "This is my house. This is my house." It was as if I had suddenly entered a crypt filled with ghosts. Dozens of blank, tired eyes looked up at me. Everyone was in handcuffs. Some people were sitting on long benches, others were sprawled out across them. A few were lying on newspapers on the ground. Half the men were asleep.

Most of the cops on the other side were white. Most of the prisoners with me were black. It seemed incongruous, and it made me stand out badly. Desperate to become less conspicuous, I found a spot near the end of a bench and sat down. *Shut up. Keep your nose clean.* I figured that if I was silent, nobody would hassle me. I imagined different scenarios of how I would defend myself if someone attacked me: throw an elbow, kick the groin, do whatever worked. But no one seemed to care about me. My fear subsided a bit. I looked around the room. One man was facing a wall, speaking to himself in Spanish. Every few minutes he'd take a couple of steps back, then a couple of steps forward to the same spot. Another man, on the opposite side of the room, sat on the floor and laughed out loud. There were no windows anywhere, just stone walls and iron bars. *Somewhere beyond this cage the sun is rising.* I needed sleep. I walked across the urine to an empty bench where I had more space to lie down and closed my eyes.

* * *

"Goldstein, Niles! Goldstein, Niles!" I woke with a shudder. A policewoman (the first woman I'd seen since the nightclub) was calling me from a corner of the room. A windowlike shutter had been pulled up from the middle of the bars opposite me. I walked over to it. The woman sat behind a table on the other side with a pile of forms in front of her. She asked me some questions about my personal history, and in five minutes it was over. I sat down again. It was a while before my name was called again, this time along with the names of about ten other prisoners. We all got up and formed a line at the door. After it was opened for us, we filed out, one by one, behind an officer. We shuffled through Central Booking silently. Some of the other cops stopped their work to watch us. Most just went about their tasks.

We came to a small room and were told to stop. A minute later another cop entered the room in front of a group of four women. Two of them appeared out of place. As I looked at them more carefully, I saw that they were transvestites. All four were prostitutes. "Every hour you keep me here," said one to the cop, "I lose money. You're ruining my business!" He told her to keep quiet. A third officer now entered the room. He held in his hand a long chain with individual handcuffs attached to it. The other two cops proceeded to remove the cuffs we were already wearing, and for a moment all of us were standing in the room with our arms free. I wondered why nobody made a run for it. But where to? The cop with the chain came up to each one of us and clamped on one of the cuffs to our right wrists. Soon we were connected. A chain gang.

We were led toward a rear exit. As I walked through it, I suddenly found myself outside. I was blinded by the sun. I had no idea what time it was. The gaping doors of a police wagon were swung open before us. My shackles rattled as I stepped up from the pavement into the vehicle. The first prisoners inside it got to sit on a bench, but the rest of us had to stand. The doors slammed shut behind us. It was hard to see. Everyone looked shadowy. While the wagon sped through the city, those of us who were standing bounced off the walls like sides of beef. No one spoke much, except the two transvestites, who talked to each other about the previous night. A man next to me began to fidget, and I could tell he was about to say something. "Somebody shut those faggots up!" he shouted finally. The other prisoners started laughing. The whole thing was pathetic.

The wagon slowed down and came to a halt. Through air vents in the side of the vehicle, I saw that we were about to enter yet another colossal structure, the Manhattan Criminal Court Building. The doors flew open and we were led inside. Once there, we were forced up against a wall in a dimly lit hallway. A bald man, this one even bigger than the one with the rubber gloves, approached us. He wore the gray uniform of a corrections officer instead of the blue of the NYPD cops we had seen. He passed a stack of yellow envelopes down our line, and I took out the one with my name and number on it. He told us to open them. Inside were my shoelaces, belt, comb, and cash. The bald man walked up to each of us, grimaced inches from our faces, and took off our handcuffs. "Let's go," he said.

We followed him down a flight of old stairs. At the bottom, the women and the transvestites were separated from the rest of us and taken away by a grim-looking policewoman. We turned right and descended another flight of stairs. "Move it," the bald man barked. The walls, which at one time were probably bone white, were now freckled with blotches of brown and yellowish filth. The bald man stopped at an imposing metal door. As it creaked open, its echo flooding the hallway, we began moving again, ducking under the door and passing into yet another corridor. *What kind of a place is this?* As if he heard my thought, the prisoner behind me, a tall man wearing a Mets cap, whispered near my ear: "You're in the Tombs."

The Tombs. I'd heard about the place before, the labyrinth of holding cells beneath the courtrooms above our heads. It was the limbo of New York's penal system. From here you waited to see a judge, and then you were either released onto the streets or sent to Rikers Island until your trial. Oddly, I no longer felt out of place—I was in the Tombs for a reason. But it didn't seem like punishment. More like a revelation. I'd descended not only into the bowels of the building, but into a dark mirror of my own soul. We reached a wall of iron bars. On the other side were more prisoners. The door slid open and the bald man said, "Get in," giving each of us a forceful nudge forward. The instant the door slid closed behind us, everyone rushed for empty benches. I hesitated. Within seconds all of the free spots were taken, and I was left standing with two or three others. The room looked similar to the other pens I'd been in, but somehow it seemed different, more exaggerated: the walls were filthier, the floors wetter, the stench thicker. Two naked lightbulbs hung from the ceiling. In one corner was a toilet and a sink. Both were smeared with human feces.

I turned toward the door and sat with my back against the bars. There were a couple of dozen prisoners in the room before we had entered it; now the room was crowded with over thirty of us. Many were smoking cigarettes. A few spoke with each other, some were sleeping. Most just sat silently or gazed at the ground. One man, wrapped in a bundle of gray rags, was lying alone on the floor, talking quietly to himself. His lips moved slowly as he spoke, but what he said was completely inaudible. He was on his back, staring at the ceiling. I watched him for an hour.

A guard suddenly appeared at the door. "Head count!" he shouted at us. Everyone in the room rose in unison and formed a line. "If you want to eat," said someone next to me, "move your ass." As soon as I stood up, the line started moving. A door I hadn't noticed before, farther down the wall, had been opened, and another guard was stationed just on the other side of it. We shuffled forward in miniature steps, as if our feet were still in shackles. The line progressed slowly. Nobody spoke. One by one each prisoner walked out of the cell, was counted by the guard, shuffled back along the outside of the bars to the main door, was handed his meal, and then silently entered the cell again. We marched in a circle, in and out of the cell, like a single piece of machinery. I found a spot on one of the benches and sat down to eat. I'd been given a plastic bag and a cup of tea. Inside the bag was one packet of sugar and two stale sandwiches. Each had one slice of cheese or one slice of meat inside it.

When everyone had returned to the cell, the iron doors slammed shut again. People immediately began to barter their meals: a packet of sugar for a cigarette; a quarter for a cheese sandwich; a cup of tea for a slice of bread. I'd never before seen people devour food the way they did in that cell. In a blind frenzy. After I took a bite out of my cheese sandwich I felt nauseous. As hungry as I was, I couldn't eat. I asked the person next to me, a somber, bearded man, if he wanted my other sandwich. He accepted it without a word. I tried to drink the tea, but it tasted like ashes. I asked the man if he would watch my place. He nodded. I got up and walked over to the sink. I spilled the tea into the sink, already brown with human waste. After turning on the faucet, I rinsed out my cup and filled it with water. I had no idea where the liquid came from, but I had to put something into my stomach. I thanked the man for guarding my spot and sat down again. "Want my sugar, too?" I asked him. He nodded.

Hours passed. I was living in pure time, and I hated it. No distractions, no tasks, no appointments, nothing. Just breathing. I imagined what it would be like to serve time on Rikers Island or in some other prison. I'd go crazy. Days, weeks, years of nothing, nothing but feeling my life slowly seep out of me. I could think of no worse torture for myself, a person enraged by his own mortality. I thought of a verse from a Delmore Schwartz poem ("Time is the fire in which we burn") and repeated it in my mind over and over again, a mantra of madness. Time felt so raw, so palpable, that I could almost cup it in my hands. I wanted to squeeze the life out of it like a trapped sparrow.

"Look at him," said a voice to my right. It was the man I'd given my sandwich to. "Just look at that guy alone on the floor." He gestured toward the man bundled in rags.

"I see him," I answered. "I noticed him before."

"Look closely," he urged me. "Take a look at his face."

"What about it?"

"He's at peace, man. He doesn't look happy or sad. He's in his own world."

The man in rags continued to talk to himself. "I wonder what he's saying?" I asked.

"He's holding a conversation with himself. It doesn't really matter what he's talking about. We probably wouldn't be able to understand him anyway."

"You're right."

"Everyone in this cell," he went on, "every single person here, has got serious troubles and worries. Not him, man. Not in the same way. I wish I could climb inside his brain for just an hour."

The two of us were bonding over a man trapped in a cage within a cage. There was something very strong in my neighbor's voice, something resolute. I trusted him.

He looked me in the eyes. "So what did you do?"

I hesitated. Compared with the crimes that the others in the room had probably committed, mine felt a little pathetic. But I told him the truth.

He chuckled. "That's all? Shit, I thought you might have killed somebody."

"Why would you think that?"

"Because you look mad as hell. That's the reason nobody's hassled you here."

I was surprised. I thought I'd been keeping a straight face the whole time.

"Listen, man," he said, "thanks for the food. I just wasn't sure about you, that's all. You'll be back on the streets in a few hours."

I wasn't sure why I believed him, but I did. I figured that at this point it was out of my hands anyway. My anger and fear had turned into fascination.

"Me, on the other hand," he continued, "I think I'm facing time again. I already spent seven years on the Island for stealing taxis. But I've been clean for five years."

"What happened?"

"Nothing, man. My downstairs neighbor borrowed a chair from me and never gave it back. When I went down and started yelling at her, she called the police on me. Charged me with assault. *Assault.* With my previous record, man, I'm afraid they'll send me back to the Island."

No one in prison is ever guilty of anything. I learned that right away. Everybody has some other explanation for why they're under lock and key: mistaken identity, frame-up, wrong place at the wrong time, you name it. But I believed him.

"Still," he continued, "it's worse here than on Rikers. At least there you know how long you're in for. You've got a bed to sleep on and real food. Here you don't know a thing. Nobody tells you anything. Not even what time it is. You just sit and wait for the judge. Sit and wait. And the guards? They're in the next room. They don't give a goddamn about what happens in here. They let us fight it out like animals. I've seen people carried out of these cells."

I wanted to get the hell out of the Tombs. I wanted fresh air, a judge, freedom. I doubted they'd send an Ivy League student with no criminal record to Rikers Island for destroying a urinal, but I was beginning to go stir crazy.

"Look," the man said, reaching into his shirt and extracting two small books. One was a pocket version of the Bible and the other a book of word pronunciations. "Books are what got me by the last time I was on Rikers. All I did was read. These are what I'm reading now. I'm not one of those religious nuts, man, but there's some great shit in the Bible. It's taught me how to live. You should check it out sometime. The other book's taught me how to speak. If you can't communicate, man, you're all alone in the world."

Just then someone stood up and started screaming. Earlier he had been sitting silently on the opposite side of the cell. Now he was hysterical. He screamed about Jesus and the Bay of Pigs, about crack, pot, pills, and speed. None of it made any sense. "I need my medicine!" he howled. "Take me to a hospital!" Everyone was staring at him except the man in rags, who continued to look up at the ceiling. The screamer reached down to the floor and picked up a handful of cigarette butts. He put them in his mouth, let out a muffled shout about his medicine, and then swallowed them. As he proceeded to writhe and gag on the ground, two guards appeared, entered the room, and dragged him out. All of us sat blankly as if nothing out of the ordinary had occurred.

More hours went by. More fire in which to burn. Yet something had changed, some feeling other than rage or fear was fermenting inside of me. I no longer wanted just to get out of the prison. I wanted to get the prison out of *me.* I was beginning to realize that unless I could learn to accept, even embrace, my humanity—with all its boundaries, imperfections, and transience—I would doom myself to carry this cell with me for the rest of my life, to wear it like an exoskeleton. I'd been given a glimpse of my inner world and its consequences. It was a revelation of darkness, but a revelation nonetheless. I couldn't win in a battle to cast off my limitations. My craving for "freedom" would mutate into a sentence of spiritual imprisonment, a living death for as long as my body endured. True liberation wasn't about boundless choice or unfettered possibility. It was about exactly the opposite.

After another head count and meal, the guards started to call out the names of people in the cell. *Call me,* I prayed, *call me.* Two or three prisoners got up and were escorted one at a time out of the room. Then a few more. About an hour later I heard my own name. A wave of excitement coursed through me. I sprang to my feet almost instantaneously and made for the door. Before I left the holding pen, I glanced back at the bearded man who'd helped to guide me through this journey into the shadows. He was looking at me, too. Neither of us said a word.

What happened next occurred very quickly, almost like a blur. A guard led me up several flights of stairs and placed me into yet another cell, this time by myself. *What now?* But within minutes a steel slit slid open and I was sitting face-to-face with a representative from legal aid, my public defender. "Tell me what you did," he said. I explained everything to him. He spoke very little, asking me a question here and there. A few minutes later he told me he'd meet me in the courtroom and closed the slit. Another guard led me down a hallway and through a large door. It was like climbing out of a pit and into a garden: the room was filled with paintings, curtains, lamps, even an American flag. After more than twenty-four hours in sensory-deprivation chambers, I was a little overwhelmed. I stood before the judge, an African American woman in a black robe who sat high above me. The prosecutors had met with my lawyer, and they were going to let me off easy since I was a first-time offender and a college student. Five minutes later I received an adjournment in contemplation of dismissal (which meant that my charges would essentially be thrown out if I stayed out of trouble for the next six months), shook my defender's hand, and stepped out of the courthouse and back onto the streets of Manhattan. But as I walked toward the curb to hail a taxi, I thought of the bearded man and all the rest of the ghosts in the Tombs beneath my feet, waiting.

After college graduation, I moved to Boston and spent the next year writing a novel. My brush with the void had shaken me, but I was determined to learn from it. I took the advice of the bearded man and read the Torah in its entirety. I read it not as literature, but as sacred text, as a living document that represented my people's response to the reality and redemptive power of God. I had experienced that power for myself in jail, but in a strange way. What I saw there initially was God's *absence*, a vision of existence preoccupied with self. It was a nightmare. But it was also a gift, a revelation. I knew I couldn't find purpose and meaning through my own efforts. Like Jacob, whose inner conflicts leave him desolate and alone with only a stone to cushion his head as he lies down to sleep; like Moses, whose rage drives him to kill an Egyptian, punish his people, and spend his days in isolation; like many others then and now, I needed a higher power to help me channel—and change—my darker impulses, to guide me away from the void and toward the Promised Land.

I had never even considered being a rabbi until this time. *Me? The hell raiser?* Yet I sensed that something was starting to shift inside me, that some new force was directing me toward an unknown but inevitable destination. In addition to reading the Torah every night, I also met with a local rabbi and had long conversations with a friend of mine who was a priest studying in Cambridge. I attended services at a nearby *havurah* (informal prayer community) and the Harvard Hillel (the Jewish student union). All of these experiences, taken together, made me open to religion as a way of life, not just as an institution within it. Though I had grown up in a home with a strong sense of Jewish identity, this was different. I wanted to explore my faith in much greater depth, to see how my life fit into it as much as it fit into my life.

It was during that year in Boston that I wrote my first book and was accepted to rabbinical school. It was more of a leap than a step. And it seemed more the result of an interior compulsion than of rational deliberation. I was becoming a rabbi because I *had* to. A large part of the process was linked to a sense of gratitude. I felt on some level that it was God who had revealed to me the full implications of the path I had been on, the path of paralysis and spiritual death. I wanted to replace self-absorption with divine service. I wanted to teach others what I had learned and to learn from the words of those teachers who had come before me. I owed God my devotion, if not my very soul.

It can take confinement to make us experience rebirth, submersion into dark waters before we can rise again. Imprisonment and descent, whether physical or existential, have sometimes been the sites of spiritual epiphanies, the contexts from which our souls are redeemed. This is one of the most powerful teachings of the Bible as well as of the Jewish and Christian traditions. Take the case of the prophet Jonah. Called by God to proclaim judgment against the city of Nineveh for its sins, Jonah flees instead to the port of Jaffa, then boards a ship for Tarshish. From the initial verses of the biblical story, as the burden of prophecy hangs over him like a colossal weight, Jonah enters a world of spiritual darkness. He doesn't just run from his responsibility. He *descends.* The Bible says that Jonah "went down" (*va-yeired* in Hebrew) to Jaffa, "went down" into the hold of the ship, went down into the sea, and descended still further into the belly of a great sea monster. The repetition of these words and images isn't accidental. It is meant to convey the prophet's spiritual fall.

Jonah's descent into the heart of darkness leads to his metaphorical death, a death that nearly becomes physical. All of his weaknesses, limitations, failures, and fears collapse in on him, threaten to crush his soul and condemn him to a living hell. Yet death (or those forces that thwart and immobilize his life) becomes the reality he must confront before he can transform his soul, before he finds the strength and courage to heed his call and fulfill his mission. His entombment, which is ultimately self-constructed and a mirror of the state of his soul, is the grim and painful truth he must confront before new life is possible.

Drowning in the spiritual abyss that has become his prison, Jonah finds redemption. He addresses God only after he has sunken "to the belly of Sheol," to the depths of despair as deep as "the base of the mountains." Jonah finds God not on the windswept peak of some majestic summit, not in a place of beauty or comfort, but at the edge, in a realm of anxiety, shadows, and muck. In the eighteenth century Elijah, the Gaon of Vilna, one of the great masters of the Jewish tradition, interprets the story of Jonah as an allegory for the journey of the soul from spiritual death to renewed life. To the Gaon, the fish that swallows Jonah represents the angel Dumah (which in Hebrew means "silence"), ruler of the netherworld. Here, Jonah—like most of us—must face his demons and fears in quietude and isolation. When he has confronted them honestly, when he has purified his soul of narcissism, God "brings up" Jonah's life from the pit into which it has fallen. The fish/Dumah, at the command of God, deposits Jonah on "dry land," which to the Gaon represents the mystical Garden of Eden, where the soul is transformed and resurrected. For Jonah, the waters of death become a wellspring of new life.

Psalm 69 utilizes this image of water to transmit a similar message about descent and ascent, death and renewed life: "Deliver me, O God, for the waters have reached my neck; I am sinking into the slimy deep and find no foothold; I have come into the watery depths; the flood sweeps me away." Here is a person at the end of his rope, someone suffocating with despair. We don't know from the text exactly *why* he is in this terrible frame of mind, why his soul is trapped in a state of such darkness, but we do know that he is in desperate need of rescue, that he can't swim on his own. The motifs and metaphors the author uses to describe his psychic situation are almost identical to those used by Jonah.

Despite the waters that have enveloped and threatened his soul, he directs his prayer to God: "Rescue me from the mire; let me not sink; let the floodwaters not sweep me away; let the deep not swallow me; let the mouth of the Pit not close over me." In the face of profound spiritual crisis, he understands that he must first acknowledge and accept his own limitations, even powerlessness, before he has a hope of finding salvation. Though the waters represent, on one level, the constraints on human capacity, on another level they serve as the catalyst for inner change and redemption. The author seems to sense this truth when he closes the psalm with the following words: "Let heaven and earth praise God, the seas, and all that moves in them. For God will save Zion, and rebuild the cities of Judah." Just as water is neutral—a substance that can kill or enliven, trap or liberate—so too are the revelations/reflections of our inner selves. What matters is how we respond to them. They can paralyze us with rage, fear, or despair, but they can also inspire us toward a better, more spiritual, God-centered existence.

John of the Cross (1542–1591) is one religious figure who understood firsthand the darkness of spiritual descent. Juan de Yepes was born into poverty in Fontiveros, a small Spanish town northwest of

Avila, and raised by a widowed mother. After moving with her to a much larger city, Medina del Campo, Juan spent the next several years working at a local hospital and attending classes at a nearby Jesuit school. These studies ignited the spiritual fire that would burn within him for the rest of his life. When he was twenty-one Juan was offered ordination to the priesthood and the position of chaplain at his hospital, but he turned down the offer and decided instead to enter the Carmelite order, which had a monastery in Medina. His attraction to solitude and the contemplative life was profound and obvious. It was during the following years, while he continued his religious studies at the University of Salamanca, that Juan met Teresa of Avila and grew interested in her efforts to reform the Carmelites and return them to a more contemplative and primitive (or "discalced") way of life. In 1568, as Juan de la Cruz (John of the Cross), he took his vows with the Reformed Carmelites and spent the next ten years living the simple life of a country monk, working, praying, and hearing confessions from Carmelite sisters at their convent in Avila.

All that would change dramatically. Teresa, John, and the other reformers were viewed as rebels by the religious authorities of their time, and the political climate toward them grew more and more hostile. John himself was denounced to the Inquisition. On the night of December 2, 1577, John was blindfolded and kidnapped by a group of friars who dragged him off to the monastery at Toledo. He was imprisoned there for the next nine months, confined to a dark, cramped cell, and punished for his disobedience. During this period, John (who was slight of build and under five feet tall) was fed little more than bread and water, permitted no change of clothing, and flogged repeatedly by his unreformed Carmelite brothers. As a result of these beatings, his shoulders were crippled for the rest of his life. Despite the severity of his imprisonment, John found some solace by composing poems in his head. This confrontation with the void of spiritual descent led to "The Dark Night of the Soul."

His escape from prison was just as dramatic as the kidnapping nine months earlier. Using strips of cloth taken from his shirt and blanket, the emaciated monk let himself down from a high wall of the monastery and fled into the night. He was taken in and sheltered by Teresa's nuns in Toledo, where he immediately began to dictate his poetry. Fearing that John might be recaptured if he remained in Toledo, the nuns sent him to an isolated mountain hermitage in a rugged region of Andalusia. There, over the next few years, he wrote his great poems, as well as his own commentary on them in which he tried to explicate their theological and mystical meanings. His insights from behind bars are clearly reflected in his worldview.

The idea of night is critical to understanding the full import of John's most famous poem, "The Dark Night of the Soul." It is not just a background image, but the very means by which a human being may encounter God. The spiritual path begins in a place of discomfort, as John explains when he interprets the first stanza:

Once in the dark of night
when love burned bright with yearning, I arose
(O windfall of delight!)
and how I left none knows—
dead to the world my house in deep repose.

The dark night, according to John, comes in two forms, the "night of sense" and the "night of the spirit." Both of these events relate to the life of the soul and are the consequence of inner contemplation—brought on through solitude, prayer, and existential struggle. The first kind of night occurs when we least expect it. It is experienced as privation and death, as a difficult and painful process of purgation.

Just when we think we have it all together, "God turns all this light of theirs into darkness," John writes in his commentary on the poem's first verse. Certainty collapses into ambiguity. Self-confidence slides into self-doubt. For God, our spiritual growth requires that God exercise tough love, stepping back and leaving us to walk a while on our own two feet. It is disorienting and terrifying. We feel abandoned, as though we've been left alone to die. God sets our souls in this dark night in order to wean us away from our attachments to the world, to purify us before we continue the spiritual journey. The night of sense is a night of purification, of mental and emotional suffering. We can only imagine the sensation of isolation and emptiness that rippled though John's soul as he sat alone in his barren cell.

Many of us never make it out of these straits. Our pain feels overwhelming and our sense of God's absence too profound. "That which this anguished soul feels most deeply," writes John, "is the conviction that God has abandoned it, that He has cast it away into darkness as an abominable thing." But if we ride out this rite of mystical passage, what at first seemed like a black hole can lead us to the second type of night, the "night of the spirit." John explains that "although this happy night brings darkness to the spirit, it does so only to give it light in everything; although it humbles it and makes it miserable, it does so only to exalt it and to raise it up; and, although it impoverishes it and empties it of all natural affection and attachment, it does so only that it may enable it to stretch forward, divinely." The purgation of our senses leads to the emptying of our soul and mind, to a state of passivity that makes room for the indwelling of God, for "the light which is to be given to it is a Divine light of the highest kind, which transcends all natural light, and which by nature can find no place in the understanding."

In the heart of darkness, where human faculties and effort fail, John of the Cross discovers the divine presence and experiences spiritual transformation. The same dark night that disintegrates his soul *re*integrates it in a new form, illuminated by the light of divine knowledge that no human intellect can comprehend. John's imprisonment in Toledo must have helped to shape his religious mind-set. The "happy" night he describes above promises us new worlds of possibility, even when life is at its worst. His receptivity to the redemptive power of such difficult and discomforting experiences leads John to faith and inner liberation, and he concludes "The Dark Night of the Soul" with a stanza that expresses this sentiment:

> *I stayed, not minding me;*
> *my forehead on the lover I reclined.*
> *Earth ending, I went free,*
> *left all my care behind*
> *among the lilies falling and out of mind.*

Two centuries after John of the Cross, another great mystic, Rabbi Shneur Zalman of Lyady (1745–1813), had a similar encounter with imprisonment. Born in Belorussia, Shneur Zalman was immersed early on in the world of traditional Jewish learning and demonstrated his exceptional intellectual gifts, mastering the entire Talmud with all of its major commentaries and codes by the time he was eighteen. After his marriage in 1760, Shneur Zalman devoted himself to religious study with even more fervor, eventually emulating many of his contemporaries and going into self-imposed "exile" by moving from Vitebsk, where he was living, to Mezeritch, the home of Rabbi Dov Baer (whose life and religious thought I will examine more fully in chapter 3) and the intellectual and spiritual center of the burgeoning hasidic movement.

His motivation was simple. A scholar who was superior to most of his peers in ability and achievement, Shneur Zalman nevertheless felt that he was deficient in his religious training and spiritual development. He thought that his mind had superseded his heart, that he had learned to serve God with his reason, through study and understanding, but not with his soul, through prayer and meditation. Rabbi Dov Baer, the leader of the Hasidim and himself an outstanding talmudic scholar, saw in Shneur Zalman a young man of great promise and made him part of his inner circle of disciples. He regularly offered him private instruction in the Kabbalah and transmitted to him the teachings that he had learned from his own spiritual master, the Baal Shem Tov. Shneur Zalman became an important new voice in this mystical movement, ultimately beginning his own hasidic system and dynasty, known today as Habad.

By the late eighteenth century tensions between the followers of Hasidism and the traditional rabbinic establishment (known as the Mitnagdim) began to emerge. The tremendous rise in popularity of Hasidism among the Jewish masses was becoming a threat to rabbinic dominance, and Hasidism itself was scorned and denigrated as anti-intellectual, even heretical. With his extensive background in traditional learning, Shneur Zalman presented himself as a bridge and peacemaker between the Hasidim and the Mitnagdim, at one point in 1774 trying (and failing) to secure a meeting with the Gaon of Vilna, one of the most respected and important rabbinic leaders of their day. During the next two decades these tensions started to boil over, sometimes violently, and Shneur Zalman, now viewed as one of Hasidism's key figures, became a target of mitnagdic contempt.

A last-ditch strategy of some of the Mitnagdim to curb the spread of Hasidism was to inform on its followers to the Russian government. In 1798 the rabbi of Pinsk formally accused Shneur Zalman of personal acts of treason against the state (he had sent charity to Palestine, which the rabbi interpreted as "helping the Turkish sultan") and of creating a new religious sect (since all sects were forbidden in Russia). Shneur Zalman was arrested and brought to trial in St. Petersburg. He spent time in prison and was later acquitted and released. But three years later he was arrested again on the same accusations and imprisoned once more. After Alexander I succeeded to the throne in 1801, Shneur Zalman was released and moved from St. Petersburg to the town of Lyady, where he spent most of the remainder of his days.

Shneur Zalman's life and religious work seemed to change after his experiences in prison. He viewed his confinement as the result not of human slander, but rather of God's displeasure with his own failure to properly and clearly transmit the teachings of Hasidism. Shneur Zalman resolved to rectify the problem. The length, depth, and exactitude of his private discourses and public lectures during the Lyady period grew more pronounced. Kabbalistic theosophy and religious ethics became the main focal points of his efforts. His disciples transcribed his words into the pamphlets and books that were to become his legacy.

Just before his imprisonment, Shneur Zalman had written in his masterwork, the *Tanya,* that every painful experience, even though its apparent cause is a human agent, is in truth connected to God, who is the Source of everything. All apparent evil, including human suffering, is in actuality a hidden, mysterious, and higher form of good. Like a pointillist painting, whose anarchic dot scheme becomes orderly and beautiful only when viewed from a distance, those experiences that seem arbitrary and ugly to us as they are happening are really essential parts of a meaningful and sacred harmony when seen from the cosmic perspective. There is no such thing as evil. There is only God, who, as the Jewish liturgy informs us, "fills the whole world with His glory." For Shneur Zalman, false imprisonment is not bad in itself, but a spiritual challenge, a descent into the abyss in order to redeem from it the sparks of holiness. With this mystical vision, he saw his time in prison as a revelation into his own inadequacies, a tool he could use for his own religious growth.

Shneur Zalman writes in the *Tanya* that the purpose of human creation in this world is to test our faith through trials and challenges. If a person believes that an absolutely good Creator is constantly involved in all of creation, even when he or she is suffering, and that everything is ultimately good, even though it is not always perceived as such, then that person should conclude that his or hers is the best of all possible situations and be satisfied with life. This is an extremely difficult task (especially in a prison cell), but Shneur Zalman claims that it becomes easier if we strive for *bitul,* or the negation of selfhood. To bemoan our hardships or lust after mundane pleasures demonstrates that we are concerned not with God's plans, but with ourselves. True spirituality is about self-surrender, about bringing our wills into alignment with the will of God. Not about the cessation of pain.

Throughout history there have been many cases—some of them famous—of people experiencing spiritual conversions or finding God while under lock and key. As moderns, our tendency is often to write off these accounts, to treat them with the same flippancy as the notion that "there are no atheists in foxholes." But my own experience in jail, as well as my studies of the Bible and of various religious figures, confirms for me at least that something does happen when our souls hit rock bottom, when we are trapped in prisons that are sometimes of our own making and are not always constructed of iron and steel. We become more attuned to our external constraints, more aware of our inner limitations, more eager for and receptive to a world beyond our walls. How we grow from these experiences depends on who we are as individuals, on our psychological makeup and personal circumstances. If we are open to their transformative power, they can deepen and enrich our lives and reshape forever the way we view reality.

There is a kabbalistic concept called *yeridah lifney ha-aliyah,* "descent before ascent." For the mystics, a journey into the abyss is a sacred rite of passage, the furnace through which our destinies are forged. Descent is a necessary, but not sufficient, experience in the life of a seeking, sensitive person. It does not have to be as dramatic as that of John of the Cross or Shneur Zalman, but it usually has a concrete context. In the biblical context, Egypt (*mitzraim* in Hebrew) serves as a metaphor for that descent, and some of the Bible's greatest heroes pass through it, all by divine design. A famine drives Abraham there but also sets into motion the birth of a people. Joseph, having first been thrown into a pit by his jealous brothers, is taken there by Midianite traders, where he later becomes a key figure in the royal court and the savior of his family. And as we know from the spiritual "Go Down, Moses," the future leader and liberator of the Israelite nation, the only human being to know God face-to-face and survive, has to initially descend "way down to Egypt land."

To make this message applicable to our own inner expeditions, we must reread the word *mitzraim* not as the historical Egypt, but as the straits of spiritual imprisonment (*metzarim*). Whether we are terrified of death, in the throes of a depression, or paralyzed by an addiction, life can sometimes feel like a cage from which there is no escape. But we all fall down. Descent is only the preparation for the ascent. To stay is to die. Abraham leaves Egypt for the land of Canaan (the Promised Land), and Moses leaves it for the wilderness of Sinai (the place of the eternal covenant between God and Israel). Even Joseph, who lives out his life in Egyptian exile, has his bones gathered and "taken up" with the Israelites during their exodus from the land of bondage. For them and for us, beyond the crucible of spiritual darkness is the light of inner redemption. If we believe that a descent into the abyss will not last forever and can ultimately make us stronger, we will outlive these nightmares. The challenge is to brave our dark nights and wait for the dawn.

2 / strange fire

He had made that last stride, he had stepped over the edge, while I had been permitted to draw back my hesitating foot. And perhaps in this is the whole difference; perhaps all the wisdom, and all truth, and all sincerity, are just compressed into that inappreciable moment of time in which we step over the threshold of the invisible.

JOSEPH CONRAD, *Heart of Darkness*

Several months before I began rabbinical school in Israel, my father called me from Chicago (at my mother's suggestion) and proposed that we take a trip to Nepal. I was twenty-two and in the middle of writing the Great American Novel, but I didn't mind the interruption. I welcomed the prospect of the two of us trekking together through the rugged and remote mountain kingdom, a father and son bonding in the shadow of Everest. My experience in the Tombs, even though it was brief, had shaken me up; the claustrophobic memory of my arrest and incarceration had intensified my desire to venture to the far corners of the world.

We flew west, spending a night in Bangkok and arriving in Kathmandu the next day. I somehow sensed that a collision was about to take place between my modern mind-set and Nepal's ancient rites. As an Ivy League graduate and a student of philosophy and literature, I had studied some of the greatest works in the Western canon: *The Republic* and *The Confessions, The Inferno* and *Paradise Lost.* I felt as though I had a good grasp of concepts like truth, virtue, and justice, of the way an "enlightened" mind could use reason and rational argument to justify the basic principles of religion and religious belief. I had to. I was going to become a modern rabbi for a modern world. But what happens when we are confronted with rituals and beliefs that seem archaic, even savage—that seem to stand at the very edge of idolatry itself? From the moment my father and I stepped out of the plane onto the tarmac of Kathmandu's airport, it was as if we had entered a different world, a land of spiritual exotica that was as seductive as it was discomforting.

During our initial descent, we saw the Himalayas—including Mount Everest—through the portholes of our plane. The legendary range was massive and bone white, a row of gigantic shoulders that looked as if they were holding up heaven. After we landed, however, what struck me most about Nepal wasn't its mountains but its colors. We stayed at a beautiful, British-era hotel called the Yak and Yeti and spent several days roaming through some of the city's less touristy markets and bazaars. We saw heaps of spices in bright colors that I had never before associated with food; stacks of sweets and meats covered with flies but—somewhat strangely—visually enticing; piles of scarves and robes in deep reds and lush greens. Even the shops that were geared toward foreigners were filled with color, a remnant of Kathmandu's psychedelic past as a major pilgrimage stop along the hippie hajj. (It was a past that resurfaced every now and then as locals would intermittently offer us mushrooms or LSD.)

There were shrines everywhere: in the middle of bazaars, at intersections, in the corners of alleyways. I could not believe the degree to which religious and civic life were intertwined in Nepal. It seemed as commonplace for people to light votive candles or place food or coins in a bowl before some painted figure of a god as it did for them to go shopping for toiletries. And it was all done so casually. As if spirituality were no big deal, just a part of daily life. Occasionally we would pass a Buddhist monk or two, bald and dressed in vivid saffron robes. While they stood out in bold relief in the crowds, they were treated by people with the same nonchalance that the shrines received. The monks reminded me of the Masai, the nomadic tribesmen I had met when I was traveling through Kenya three years earlier (though their robes were bright red). To me the monks were exotic; to the average resident of Kathmandu they were simply ordinary fixtures of the city.

Some of the monks studied in their religious academies, while others walked around the perimeters of the temples, spinning tiny prayer disks built into a wall as they passed. We saw one monk standing alone, a small prayer wheel turning in his hand, wearing an enormous ritual head covering that pointed straight toward the sky. He was mouthing prayers that were barely audible to us. The temples were as colorful as the markets. One temple in particular struck me as especially interesting: it had a giant, watchful eye painted on its dome. That image, combined with many of the other representations, carvings, and ornamental figures of gods with tusks, horns, and elephant snouts that we saw all over Kathmandu, started to make me feel more and more uncomfortable. There I was, a young Jew (and a proud monotheist) about to enter rabbinical school, walking among what at first blush seemed like graven images, false gods, idols. It triggered all of my worst fears and biases. It felt as if I were in the belly of thc beast.

I was torn between wanting to enjoy my visit to a remote country and wanting to shatter its statues with a baseball bat. The figures of strange gods were not the only features of the city that troubled my religious sensibilities. There were also the harems—or rather their remnants, the empty buildings that had once been used in the distant past as residences for the concubines of the region's various rulers. These too had figures on them, not of gods but of men and women copulating with each other. Each side of the harems' roofs depicted an assortment of sexual acts and positions in graphic detail.

In the Bible, the prophets constantly railed against the false gods and prostitution cults of the ancient Near East. Both were spiritual abominations to their ethical monotheism. But idolatry is a complicated issue. The line between sacrament and sacrilege is not always clear, especially when one tries to compare religions that are completely different from one another. The writings of Moses Maimonides, the great twelfth-century rabbi and philosopher, suggest that a person who outwardly performs all of the proper religious rituals and obligations could still be an idolater inside (that is, have a distorted conception of God), while a person who uses idols as tangible intermediaries could still be praying (though he or she might not be aware of it) to the one true God. Were all of those people we saw idolaters? I could not bring myself to think that. Part of me viewed their actions as expressions of profound humility, yet I never felt truly comfortable with many of the rites and representations we witnessed there.

In addition to exploring the streets and sites of Kathmandu, my father and I made a trek through the Annapurna Range, a majestic stretch of mountains just below the Himalayas. Despite my initial protestations, Sherpas carried most of our bags up and down the mountain trails. But it was a difficult journey, and my old man's stamina impressed me. Every once in a while we passed a small village, tucked away from the rest of civilization. Even in those communities religious shrines and images—as well as flasks of homemade brandy—were ubiquitous. The most jarring sight for me was a building with swastikas and Stars of David painted side by side (we learned that both images were part of the ancient religious iconography of the region).

After we had completed our trek, we rafted down a Himalayan-fed river south toward the jungle and spent a couple of nights at a strange resort called Tiger Tops. We rode into the camp through dense bush, sitting on the back of an elephant, and slept in huts that were built in the tops of tall trees. The "highlight" of our stay, which was carefully staged for the tourists by the resort's staff, was being rushed out of the camp after dinner and driven by jeep to a high fence, behind which we watched through binoculars as a Bengal tiger devoured some helpless deer that had been tied to a stake earlier in the evening.

We had only two or three days left in the country when we returned to Kathmandu. Coming to Nepal had been my father's idea. But it was my idea to watch the animal sacrifices at a shrine in the Kathmandu Valley a few hours outside the city. I had read about Dakshinkali in our guidebook, about the weekly pilgrimage of men and women from the surrounding towns and villages and the offerings they made there. I wanted to witness firsthand this bizarre, alien, and (so I imagined) grotesque event. I was unsure and anxious about just how I would feel. Would I be physically sickened? Religiously outraged? All I knew was that I had to go there to see it for myself.

The site buzzed with activity. Hundreds of people stood in line, their various animals in tow, waiting their turn. We stood in a different line, on a hill above the shrine, with other onlookers. Everybody at the complex followed the same procedure, offering prayers at the shrine, handing over the animal and a few coins to the ritual slaughterer, standing to the side as the killing took place, and then taking the carcass away for their feast. Groups of families congregated around open pits (for roasting the fresh meat) and tables on the grounds, only yards from the site of the slaughter. The blood drizzled from the courtyard down to the stream below.

The barefoot man killed with such precision that when he cut the heads off chickens it looked as though he were just snapping his fingers. One family gave him a goat. For a second or two the animal's face turned up in my direction. In its eyes was an expression of horror, a visceral understanding that it was about to die—violently and irrevocably. The goat squirmed and bleated helplessly in the slaughterer's arms. Taking out a much larger knife, the man sliced swiftly through its throat, and the goat let out a stunted scream as it was decapitated. Blood sprayed wildly from its neck; the severed head fell with a disturbing thud to the ground, rolling a few feet across the courtyard before it came to a stop on one of the dirty tiles. My father grimaced and clutched me as if his embrace would shield me from the blade. The only other time I had seen my father so outwardly moved was many years before, when he was told of his own father's death. In that uneasy embrace I felt my father's greatest fear. But I also sensed his deepest love.

The phenomenon of sacrifice, and its connection to the relationship between a father and his son, also occurs in one of the Torah's most famous and powerful passages. In chapter 22 from the book of Genesis, the patriarch Abraham receives a command from God to offer up his son Isaac on Mount Moriah. The two of them ascend the mountain in silence, and it is not until Abraham has bound his son, placed him on an altar, and lifted a knife above his throat that a second divine call prevents the slaughter. It was merely a test of faith. Isaac is rescued from death, and a ram is sacrificed instead. Though my father's outer behavior differed dramatically from that of Abraham's, the inner impulse of the two men was the same: trying to do the right thing, as they understood it, regardless of cost. Through Abraham's (aborted) attempt to sacrifice Isaac, and my father's (instinctive) attempt to protect me, both men were poised to give up that which was most precious to them. For Abraham, it was his beloved son. For my father, an emotionally inward man, it was his guard, his human vulnerability. In one rabbinic legend, Isaac's soul flies out of him in terror and he dies on the altar, but he is instantly revived by God. The event transforms him as well as the way he relates to Abraham. Since Nepal, I have never been able to read that passage from Genesis—or view my father—in quite the same way, either.

The story of the binding and attempted sacrifice of Isaac is a profoundly disturbing one, and it has been commented on for centuries by rabbis and priests, philosophers and poets. No Jew or Christian can be serious about his or her religious convictions and practices without confronting this difficult text that depicts Abraham's apparent willingness to slay his own son in the name of divine obedience. Some modern readers have noted that human sacrifice was central to the cults of Israel's neighbors, that in the context of Abraham's place and time God's request could have seemed legitimate, and that the outcome of the story is ultimately a rejection of the rite itself. But to me this whitewashes the issue. Abraham was going to kill his child. How do we make sense of the seemingly inexplicable? How can we adhere to religious traditions that hold up such a man as the very paradigm of rectitude?

It was not until I went to Dakshinkali that I started to grapple with these issues in any meaningful way. Though I had read about sacrifice in the Bible, I had to witness an actual experience of it before I could form my own opinion on the matter. Dakshinkali demonstrated the seductive dimension of sacrifice, the raw, primal power it can unleash, even for those who observe it from afar. Dakshinkali gave me a glimpse of how death could be sanctified, how religious ritual could transform simple butchery into a divine gift. Yet it also showed me its danger, for it is a spirituality rooted in violence and destruction, which holds within it a kernel of darkness. The story of Abraham and Isaac reveals the possibilities of that darkness. It was not a spirituality I could live with—it was too close to the edge, too similar to the practices and beliefs that my own tradition had eliminated so many centuries earlier. Would I be able to devote my life to a God who demanded the gift of death?

I went to the shrine at Dakshinkali with a seminarian's zeal, expecting to find a den of heathenism. What I found instead was a spirituality of sacrifice that we in the West have rightly rejected, but a spirituality that was once a vital part of my own religious tradition and the context out of which Christianity emerged. Sacrifice, the act of "making sacred," is significant not simply because it is one of the historical foundations of the Jewish and Christian traditions. It is significant because it is a spiritual value that still has much to teach us, if we handle it with caution and adapt it to our era. For some, it is through devotion to religion, such as saying the rosary or observing Sabbath prohibitions, that we sanctify life; for others, it is through inner growth, such as working with the chakras or practicing meditation. We enter dangerous territory when those paths become extreme and all-consuming. For me, *that* is the message of the Genesis story, and of the blood at Dakshinkali.

The spiritual impulse can sometimes lure us too close to the edge—so close that we risk being sucked into the void. Sometimes we skirt the line between the sacred and the sacrilegious without even knowing it. Another disturbing story from the Torah centers on the figures of Nadav and Avihu, sons of the high priest Aaron. In the book of Leviticus, we read that the two men "took each of them his censer, and put fire therein, and laid incense thereon, and offered strange fire before the Lord, which He had not commanded them. And there came forth fire from before the Lord, and devoured them, and they died before the Lord." (10:1–2) What is this "strange fire," this mysterious offering that brings about their violent deaths? The text says nothing about the nature of the offering itself. Many commentators have claimed that the real crime of Nadav and Avihu was that they had been involved in idolatrous practices, that the gift they presented to God was thus polluted through their own improper behavior and transformed from a meritorious expression of piety into a religious abomination. While their intentions might have been good, the effects of their "strange" spirituality led to annihilation. Not all forms of divine worship are acceptable. Some are merely masks that hide a crooked core. And when we play with fire, we can burn ourselves.

What to some people seem like acts of holiness can in reality be acts of horror, and there have been periods in the Christian tradition when these behaviors have surfaced in dark and disquieting ways. Nowhere is this dynamic more apparent than in the church's response to witchcraft. Sometimes the border between miracles and magic is murky, especially in many of the non-Western spiritual traditions. Whether it is shamans in Central Asia and Siberia, medicine men in the Americas, or mediums in Africa, spirituality and sorcery are often intertwined. Do these figures and practices cross the threshold of religious propriety? Or is our discomfort (such as that which I experienced myself in Nepal) merely relative, a matter of perception and bias? The Catholic Church is founded on and filled with supernatural events, from the miracles of Jesus in the New Testament to such normative institutions as the sacraments, sainthood, the sprinkling of holy water, and the Eucharist. (One of the essential differences between Protestantism and Catholicism centers on the mass; the former views it in purely symbolic terms, while the latter continues to believe in transubstantiation, the idea that during the sacred rite the wafers and wine transform into the actual body and blood of Jesus himself.) Once the early church had become an established religion, it had to distinguish between its own, acceptable miracles and the "black magic" of others, the unbelievers and heretics. A collision course was set. Radical devotion to religious boundaries would eventually lead to bloodshed.

As soon as the church had stability and power, it acted to suppress magic and witchcraft. Constantine threatened all practitioners of unauthorized black arts with severe punishment. By the eighth and ninth centuries the idea of the devil came more and more into prominence. Common religious rites took on new meanings; baptism, for instance, was regarded as a kind of exorcism, an expulsion of the evil spirit from a person's body. While in general church philosophers such as Thomas Aquinas were not excessively focused on the devil, the popular culture of the Middle Ages was rife with demonology and the belief in and fear of witchcraft, the product of the unholy union of human beings and Satan.

Some tried to harness the power of the supernatural for "good" purposes outside the confines of the church. Methods were developed for predicting the future; wands and divining rods were used to find buried treasure; magic formulas in Hebrew or Latin that invoked God, or magic symbols such as pentagrams and circles, were spoken or drawn in the hope of manipulating the natural world for some specific goal. The New Age movement today mirrors these practices. I once spent a week chasing twisters through Tornado Alley with a man who firmly believed he possessed the ability to divine which severe storm systems we ought to drive into. The philosopher Agrippa of Nettesheim (1486–1535) argued that there was a fundamental difference between black magic and what he called "natural" or "celestial" magic. For him, if the supernatural forces were utilized appropriately, they could lead to a mystical union with God—even though it took place beyond the walls of a church and through spells and ceremonies that were far removed from the Christian sacraments.

Yet no unsanctioned form of supernaturalism, however well intentioned, was ultimately acceptable to the church. And the charge of necromancy was often merged with that of heresy as a way of stifling internal dissent. One of the earliest instances of such an action occurred in 385, when Priscillian, a bishop from Spain, was tortured and together with some of his followers decapitated at Treves. As an infallible foundation for their zeal and behavior, ecclesiastical officials used verses from the Bible, such as "Thou shalt not suffer a sorceress to live" (Exodus 22:18), to justify the harsh prosecutions. The title "inquisitor," a judge in matters of religious faith, was used for the first time at the Council of Tours in 1163. The synod that met in Verona in 1184 cursed all heretics and ordered them to be turned in to the secular authorities for capital punishment. Under Innocent III (pope from 1198 to 1216), instigator of the fourth crusade, a new order of priests, the Dominicans, was created; it would be the backbone of the emerging Inquisition. After the Council of Toulouse in 1229, the Inquisition became an established church institution, overseen directly by the pope. In 1232 Gregory IX appointed the Dominicans ("hounds of the Lord" in Latin) as the official papal inquisitors.

While to us the Inquisition might seem like a very strange expression of spirituality, to the inquisitors it was a sacred duty and an act of submission to God's will. For them, union with the divine was expressed just as much through burning flesh as it was through the pages of their prayer books or the sacraments of their tradition. But there was some resistance within the church to the fanatical impulse that was beginning to drag it toward the edge of madness. When Gregory IX sent an emissary, Conrad of Marburg, to Germany, he was given absolute power to call before his tribunal any person suspected of witchcraft and the authority to have that individual burned alive. Yet Conrad was met with fierce opposition; some of the important German archbishops tried to resist his witch-hunt. One of them wrote a letter to the pope, denouncing the inquisitor and arguing, "Whoever fell into his hands had only the choice between a ready confession for the sake of saving his life and a denial, whereupon he was speedily burnt. Every false witness was accepted, but no just defense granted—not even to people of prominence." The letter fell on deaf ears. The fires of the Inquisition raged on.

While in Germany the establishment of the Holy Office (the church name for the Inquisition) encountered resistance, it was largely embraced in France. In 1275 the inquisitor Hugo de Beniols ordered a number of high-profile people burned alive in Toulouse. One of them, a sixty-five-year-old woman named Angèle, Lady of Labarthe, was accused of having had sexual intercourse with the devil. The charge stated that she became pregnant and gave birth to a monster with a wolf's head and a serpent's tail, a beast that ate nothing but babies for its food. This image of demonic creatures devouring innocent Christian babies was applied with horrifying regularity to members of the Jewish community during the Middle Ages (and, tragically for my people, beyond this time, as seen in the infamous blood libel accusations made against them), and Jews, who were viewed by many both as God-killing heretics and the seed of Satan, were frequently the special targets of zealous and bloodthirsty prosecutors. The Inquisition also thrived in Spain. Church documents from the period describe the elaborate spy system, modes of cross-examination, methods of torture, and spoils of the Spanish Holy Office. And two of the most active inquisitors, Torquemada and Ximenes, men whose names are almost synonymous with the Inquisition, belonged to the Church of Spain.

The victims of the Inquisition, for all practical purposes, had no hope of redemption. Witchcraft was viewed by the church as an exceptional crime that demanded exceptional measures. It was a great evil to which the standard laws and rules of procedure could not be applied. By the fifteenth century, torture, which had previously been used mainly in special circumstances, began to edge closer to the norm. Two of the most common torture methods were the fire and water ordeals, whereby suspects were brought to the point of death in order to solicit a "confession" from them. Other methods included thumbscrews, tongs and pincers for tearing out fingernails, Spanish boots, collars and chains, boards covered with spikes, the rack, and the Iron Maiden (a steel "virgin" whose embrace led to a slow and excruciatingly painful demise). All of this was seen as holy work.

During the Inquisition, most accusations were founded on circumstantial evidence (at best) and rooted more in irrational fears, superstitions, prejudices, and petty jealousies than in hard "proof" of witchcraft. No one was safe from its flames, especially religious reformers, thinkers (such as Galileo), and non-Christians. In the end, the response by the church to the popular witch hysteria of that time was far darker and more sacrilegious than the alleged acts of black magic and heresy themselves. It was a clear case of idolatry: blind subservience to a grotesque ideal substituted for submission to idols. In zealously trying to serve God, the church was bathed in blood for hundreds of years.

Sometimes we deify not only ideas but ourselves. One of the great legends in the Jewish tradition is that of the Golem, a mythical monster conjured from clay. It is written in the Talmud that the third-century Babylonian sage Rava created an artificial being by means of magic. There is also a legend that the medieval poet-philosopher Solomon Ibn Gabirol created a female Golem. (Due to a communicable skin disease, Ibn Gabirol had lived in total isolation, but after he was denounced to the rabbinic authorities for having created a woman for "improper" purposes, he destroyed the Golem.) Another person rumored to have created a Golem was Rabbi Elijah of Chelm, a sixteenth-century mystic. Creation of a Golem was considered the mark of a master Kabbalist, the product of esoteric rituals, mysterious incantations, and the invocation of secret names. As a literary creation its beauty and power are clear, but as a religious phenomenon the Golem myth raises a host of dire problems. For it demonstrates, as does the Inquisition much more dramatically and violently, the dangers of mingling magic with spiritual expression, as well as how easy it is to slide from sacred worship to idolatry.

While the Golem legend has deep roots in the Jewish tradition, it has become most closely associated in modern times with Rabbi Judah Loew, the Maharal of Prague (who died in 1609). The Maharal was an important thinker, mystic, and communal leader who lived midway between the classical period of the Kabbalah in medieval Spain and the hasidic movement that would emerge two centuries after his death in eastern Europe. In his youth the Maharal was educated along conventional Jewish lines, receiving a firm grounding in the legal intricacies of the Talmud. As he grew older, however, the Maharal broke with what he viewed as the spiritual sterility of this approach; he began to study the Zohar, the classic text of the Kabbalah, as well as other mystical tractates. As his reputation spread throughout the Jewish world, the Maharal attracted more and more followers to Prague, Jews who were hungry for words of wisdom from this brilliant scholar and mystic. Exactly when and how he became identified with the Golem is unclear.

According to legend, Judah Loew decided to create a huge, superhuman being, a monster without a soul. There are at least three versions of the story that seem to explain why: to be a servant in his home; to protect Prague's Jews from their enemies; to help the Maharal in fighting accusations of blood libel (ritual murder of Christian children) being made at the time against the Jewish community. The giant creature that the Maharal brought into being was an automaton, an artificial life form without a will of its own. The Golem served as a tool in its master's hands and was subject to the command of the rabbi alone. As some modern thinkers have pointed out, the Golem is in certain ways a replica of Adam, the primeval man. We read in Genesis that God created Adam from a heap of clay and infused him with the spark of divine vitality and intelligence (the "divine image"). Without this intellect and willful creativity implanted in him, Adam would have been little more than a Golem himself, a thoughtless mass of matter constructed by natural laws and forces. It is only the divine spark that transforms Adam into a true human being or, as the Torah refers to him, an image of God.

When a mystic creates a Golem, he or she is mirroring the actions of God. Therein lies the power as well as the danger of this enterprise. One of the more famous descriptions of the creation of a Golem involves none other than the Maharal himself. In a letter attributed to him, Judah Loew explains how a Golem is made:

> And I commanded my son-in-law, Rabbi Isaac ha-Kohen, to be the first to circumambulate the Golem seven times, beginning from the right side [of the feet] and up to the head, and from the head to the feet on the left side; and I gave him the combinations of letters to recite during the circumambulation. And he did so seven times, and when he finished the circumambulations the body of the Golem became red, as a burning coal of fire. Afterwards I commanded my disciple, Rabbi Yaakov Sason ha-Levi, to do seven circumabulations as well, similar [to the preceding ones] and I also gave him other combinations of letters. When he finished the circumambulations, [the Golem's] appearance had hairs, as [a person of] thirty and the nails grew at the extremities of the fingers. Then I also did the circumambulations, and after the end of the circumambulations we said together the verse: "And God blew the soul of life in his nostrils and man became a living being." (GENESIS *2:7)*

The instructions for creating a Golem are, at least according to the above passage, intricate and arcane. In characteristically kabbalistic fashion, specific (and Jewishly significant) numbers figure prominently in this description: three different rabbis, seven circles around the Golem, thirty years of age in appearance. The recitation of secret letter combinations and formulas is also a typical feature of esoteric kabbalistic rites. The ceremony is bizarre; it looks unlike any of the other rituals and rites in the normative Jewish tradition. In this scene, the Maharal is mimicking God, giving birth to a being that is fully animate and fully alive—but that lacks a soul. The Golem is not an image of God, but a *distortion* of that image. When the creature begins to come to life, he glows red like a burning coal. Is the Maharal playing with (strange) fire?

The power that Judah Loew unleashes is a reflection of God's own creative power; after having built his Golem, the rabbi thus puts a slip of paper into its mouth on which is inscribed the ineffable name of God. For as long as the mystic seal is in its mouth, the Golem can live. Yet the creature cannot speak. He can only respond reflexively to orders. In one of the legends, the Golem is given its day of rest on the Sabbath. Every Sabbath the Maharal would remove the slip of paper from the Golem's mouth, and the Golem would become inanimate and still for the duration of the day. One Friday afternoon before sunset, however, the Maharal forgot to remove the seal from the creature's mouth and went to the synagogue to pray with the Jewish community of Prague.

As dusk fell, the Golem—alone and without guidance—became restive. The creature suddenly began to grow in size and strength. As if it were insane, the Golem started to rampage in a wild frenzy throughout the Jewish ghetto, threatening to demolish anything it could lay its hands on. No one in the community knew how to bring the Golem under control, how to stop it from its violent and reckless assault. Soon word of the unfolding incident reached the synagogue where the Maharal was praying. The rabbi raced out into the street to confront the Golem, a creature that he himself had created and that now appeared to have outgrown its dependence on him and become an uncontrollable and destructive power on its own. After a great struggle, the Maharal stretched forth his hand toward the giant creature and ripped the Holy Name out of its mouth. Instantly the Golem collapsed lifelessly to the ground, nothing more than a massive mound of clay. According to legend, the remains of the Golem lie hidden to this day in the attic of the Klaus Synagogue in Prague.

While the creation of a Golem is on one level an affirmation of the creative power of human beings, the dangers of such an activity are clear. An adept Kabbalist (or the Dr. Frankenstein of Mary Shelley's famous gothic novel) might be able to manipulate the forces of nature in order to produce an animated, living being, but reason, intuition, speech, emotion—an inner soul—will always be beyond it: the being might simulate human behavior, but it will never *be* human. When, as the Talmud notes, the sage Rava sends his Golem to Rabbi Zera, and Rabbi Zera tries to converse with it and is met only with a bone-chilling silence, he exclaims to the soulless creature: "You who have been created by magic—return to your dust!" The construction of a synthetic form of life, even if it were possible, is an act of sacrilege, an unholy attempt to imitate divine work. Authentic spirituality is ultimately about our ever evolving relationship with God, one that ranges from frustration and anger to gratitude and worship. But magic, at its core, is an act of *self*-worship. It is a false spirituality, a fascinating yet troubling form of idolatry.

The Golem existed on two planes. For serious Kabbalists it was a prop for ecstatic experience, a clay figure that, when infused with the dreams and hopes of the human mind, came "alive" for a brief moment of mystical rapture. The Golem was also a tool that allowed the Kabbalist, in a ritualized way, to penetrate the mysteries of creation and become a creator himself, uniting, if only for an ecstatic instant, with the divine Creator (much as Agrippa of Nettesheim had described in his writings on celestial versus black magic). In the Jewish folk tradition, such as the previous tale that has been attributed to the Maharal, the Golem was removed from the metaphysical plane and placed in the legendary one. Rather than being a personal spiritual experience of a Kabbalist (which, since it elevated the mystic to the same level as God, was risky enough), the Golem became a supernatural creature, a physical servant to an individual's needs and desires controlled by that person uneasily and with great caution. Yet whether the Golem exists on the plane of mysticism or magic, it represents a form of religious expression that is as problematic as it is unusual. It is truly a spirituality at the edge.

Idolatry is what we find when we step over that edge. The path to God is not always level, and unless we are careful, we can easily slide from sanctity to sacrilege, from holiness to hollowness. Many of today's spiritual movements and trends seem to be hovering very close to that edge. Modern paganism is one example. We should revere the earth—not worship it, as pagans do. Another example is Wicca, which sees magic as a valid (and the original) form of spirituality. Even the Kabbalah, as it is often taught today, has been conflated with—and tainted by—astrology, crystals, and other beliefs and elements that have little or nothing to do with Judaism. These contemporary spiritualities focus on how the divine can serve *us*, not on what we owe God.

Idolatry can come in many forms: worship of self, worship of an idea, worship of a statue. What makes a spiritual expression unacceptable, even *unholy*, is not its form but its substance. If the kernel is rotten, and if the result of a particular religious act is the deification of something other than the divine, regardless of a person's apparent intention, then the odor of that offering will befoul the nostrils of God. For when faith edges toward its extremes, it can lead to some extremely interesting manifestations of the spiritual impulse. But it can also lead to strange fire, to practices and consequences that can spiral out of our control, mutate into configurations that are abominable, and plunge us into an abyss darker and more terrifying than the deepest pit.

3 / forests of the night

Tyger Tyger burning bright,
In the forests of the night:
What immortal hand or eye,
Dare frame thy fearful symmetry?

WILLIAM BLAKE, "The Tyger"

The Kenai Peninsula juts out in a wedge from the Alaskan mainland. Beyond Kenai is Kodiak Island, home to some of the largest grizzlies in North America. And beyond Kodiak are the Aleutians, a string of islands that stretches over a thousand miles across the Bering Sea. Then there is just water, ice, and emptiness. If you gaze west from the right spot at the top of one of Kenai's mountains, and you let your imagination drift with the wind and the waves, it can seem as though you are standing at the edge of the world.

I once stood in that place. It was the summer of 1989, and in a couple of months I would be moving to Jerusalem to begin rabbinical school. What was a nice Jewish boy like me doing on a mountain in the middle of nowhere? The community I would soon serve felt very far away at that moment and offered me little in the way of spiritual nourishment. If I couldn't experience God within the confines of the American Jewish establishment (which seemed much more interested in building Holocaust memorials or worrying about anti-Semitism and assimilation), I'd try to find my own religious path. Wherever that search took me.

I left for Alaska in June. For reasons that were unclear to me at the time, Alaska had taken on great dimensions in my mind and in my heart: a symbol for all that was wild, a metaphor for the untamable, the unknown, the frontier. I wasn't a stranger to hiking through the wilderness, but I'd never before experienced what I imagined to be the remoteness, or the enormity, of Alaska's majestic terrain. I'd transformed Alaska into my own dark forest and endowed it with an almost mystical quality. I wanted to fuse the call of the wild with the call of my faith. I sensed that my trip to the Land of the Midnight Sun would be far more than a summer vacation. It would be a pilgrimage.

My friend Scott picked me up in Chicago. The rear of his Jeep Cherokee overflowed with college miscellany—books, records, clothing, and a drum set. We somehow managed to squeeze in my backpack and sleeping bag and pushed off into the night. Scott was on his summer break and was going to work for the next two months at his family's peach orchard in the San Joaquin valley. The plan was for us to drive together cross-country to Seattle, where I would catch a flight up to Ketchikan, Alaska, and he would head south to California. We sped through plains, badlands, mountains, and deserts, spending our nights on the roof of his Jeep, drinking beer and watching shooting stars. Five days later, as the sun emerged over the Seattle-Tacoma Airport, the two of us went our separate ways.

For the first few weeks I wandered alone through the Inside Passage, a panhandle of islands and inlets in southeast Alaska that is accessible only by boat or plane. At the end of the month I hooked up with a group of kayakers in Gustavus, a tiny village at the mouth of the frigid waters of Glacier Bay National Park. A floatplane dropped us off deep within the preserve, and we spent a week in our kayaks, camping on various shores and islands as we made our way back out. My afternoons were filled with the spray of humpbacks and the play of harbor seals, my evenings with the moaning of the wind and the howling of wolves. Glaciers were everywhere, and the approach to them was always the same. First I would see the icebergs, floating like blue candy and sometimes as tall as houses. Then, after circumnavigating them carefully, I would hear the thunder, the distant roar of ice blocks as they cracked off the faces of glaciers and crashed into the water below. Finally, chilled by the breezes that swept over their tops, I would reach the tidewater glaciers themselves, rivers of white ice unraveling into the sea.

Soon it was time to move on. I flew north to Anchorage and took a train on the Alaska Railroad to Denali National Park. Denali is known for its physical beauty and its plentiful wildlife. It is also known for its tourists. Yet as a lover of open spaces and wild animals, I viewed Denali's rolling plains as a dream come true. Escaping the throngs at the entrance, I made my way inside the park, eventually discovering a narrow stream that cut along the base of Mount McKinley and the Alaska Range. Drawn by its beautiful setting, I followed the stream for about a mile, flanked on each side by snow-capped mountains and Arctic tundra. I offered a prayer, feeling as if I were standing in some immense temple, replete with white pillars and green carpets.

The day was clear and the air cool. I passed caribou and Dall sheep as ptarmigans darted across my path. My mind wandered from images and memories of the past year in Boston to forecasts and fantasies about the year to come in the Holy Land. The presence of wildlife was mesmerizing. Even when it was invisible, I sensed its reality. Through imprints in the soil. Droppings. Hair on broken twigs. Living beings surrounded me at every turn. Yet as hypnotic as these creatures were, it wasn't until I entered a thicket, and stomped through it into a clearing, that I was truly stunned, and stopped dead in my tracks.

At first it looked like a fuzzy golden ball, a mound of bronze shimmering in the summer sun. But this ball had legs—four of them—and as it lumbered toward me, I quickly came to realize that the fuzz was really fur, and that the object wasn't a ball, but a bear. A *grizzly* bear.

I can't describe what darted through my body as the distance between the two of us shrank, because it was beyond words. All I had at that instant was a sensation, raw, primal, and almost as palpable as the sound of the brush as it crunched under the grizzly's paws. If I had to choose a name for it, I'd call it fear. Naked, unbridled fear.

In classical Jewish thought, it is only after one has experienced the fear of God that life gains complete clarity, that a person fully and finally understands his or her place in the cosmic whole. Standing there, scared, vulnerable, and alone, in the presence of a being far more powerful and attuned to nature than I could ever hope to be, gave me a hint of what it must be like to behold the Divine Presence, to experience a brief, mystical, life-altering flash of transcendence. There is an inscription above the Holy Ark in a great many synagogues around the world—I'd seen it myself in places as different as Brooklyn, Moscow, Nairobi, and Casablanca. The Hebrew reads *Da lifney mi atah omed*: "Know before Whom you stand." But there are times in our lives when such an admonition seems unnecessary.

I had stepped back into the food chain. I felt terror, but I also felt a strange sort of reverence. As if the threat of being eaten alive were somehow tempered by the knowledge that if it occurred, it would occur not as some random or malicious act, but as an *enactment* of some grand and mysterious design. This was a situation that was beyond good and evil, beyond even reason. It was a situation that transcended all logical categories, a moment in which the whole was far greater than the sum of its parts.

Don't run. Don't stare into the bear's eyes. Keep it in your peripheral vision. Do nothing to excite the grizzly's predatory instinct, but get the hell out of there. Walk swiftly but calmly. Put as much distance as possible between yourself and the bear. I did everything I'd read that a person should do in the event of a bear encounter, but as the grizzly began following me, all my thoughts and strategies began to melt into a kind of white heat. I still had the residue of a mind, enough to keep my legs moving and my lungs filled with air, but for the first time in my life I was all body. Just a sack of blood and bones. A moveable feast.

I had had a run-in with two black bears the summer before while camping in the Upper Peninsula of Michigan. I was able to scare those bears away from my tent, and I knew that though blackies could climb trees, grizzlies couldn't. But Denali was tundra—it had no trees. There was nowhere to escape to, nowhere to hide. I was naked. With the grizzly still on my tail, I spotted a dirt road off in the distance. Turning at a 120-degree angle away from the bear (a young male that probably weighed several hundred pounds) so as to maximize the separation between the two of us, I made my way toward the road. Perhaps it would lead me to better shelter.

The bear followed me. My heart was beating so fast, it felt as if it would burst. Though I saw it indirectly, too afraid to look at it face-to-face, that grizzly had more raw presence than my own soul. Lifting my feet felt like lifting manhole covers. Every step was gravid. When I finally reached the road, I discovered two cameramen and a Jeep. The three of us jumped inside the vehicle just as the bear closed in. Something inside me snapped. Or was freed. *I'm safe! Alive!* Exhilaration and gratitude—even a vague, objectless feeling of love—began to replace fear and trembling. As the animal watched us silently from a hillside, I asked the men why they were there. They told me they were making a documentary on grizzlies.

How does the experience of confronting a wild animal relate to God? As William Blake tries to convey through the verses of his famous poem "The Tyger," the mere *fact* of such a mysterious and terrifying creature is inspirational. It also poses a question: Who, or what, possesses the deep imagination and bold power to create such a seemingly unearthly being? In this sense, Blake's tiger, like the grizzly I encountered in Alaska, is revelatory, a living monument to its Creator, a trace of the transcendent force that formed it. More than a work of art, it is a mark of divinity. Our fear of these animals is, at a deeper level, merely a mask for our awe of God.

Fear, reverence, and awe are the products of more than just visceral experience. Maimonides writes that when one reflects on the world in its totality, with its vast and complex array of beings, one immediately "trembles and grows fearful, for he becomes aware that he is a tiny and lowly creature, with meager knowledge compared to Him who possesses perfect knowledge." It is the realization of our existential situation, our humanity in the face of God's divinity, that results in these sometimes uncomfortable emotional responses. But that discomfort can serve as a gateway, breaking down our defenses and allowing the realm of the transcendent to penetrate our souls.

In the Bible, God is sometimes referred to as a "devouring fire." The Kabbalists interpret this to mean that in order for the human soul to reach its highest level of development, in order for it to experience the ecstasy of mystical union, it must first be "swallowed" by God. Like a single flame vanishing into a raging inferno, the absorption of our finitude into the infinity of God can be terrifying. Yet despite the trauma and terror that come with it, the surrender of the human ego, the sacrifice of our very sense of self to a higher power, seems to be the prerequisite for true spiritual transformation. Its catalyst is not always the same (it can be an emotional, intellectual, or mystical one), but the end result, whichever pathway we follow, is the elevation of our souls to a more profound level of relationship with God.

* * *

Whether it takes the form of awe, reverence, or terror, fear is often an integral part of spirituality. Sometimes fear precedes spiritual experience, sometimes it accompanies it, and sometimes it is the residue the event leaves behind. When we brush up against something that is far greater than us, something that almost defies our comprehension, it is not always a pleasant experience. The same can be true when we encounter the ultimate transcendent force, God. We may become distressed and scared. We may feel powerless and vulnerable. Many mystics write about the role of these feelings in their own religious encounters.

Few periods in the history of Christian mysticism in Europe rival that of the thirteenth and fourteenth centuries, a period notable not just for the depth and sophistication of its mystics, but also in their variety of voices. Women, left with few other places to go (since they were excluded by church law from active ministry and forced to the fringes of religious life), burst onto the mystical scene. Some scholars view the women mystics of this time as spiritual pioneers who helped to "feminize" what had been up to then an almost entirely male domain. God was no longer described using only masculine language and imagery. Metaphors for mystical experience now reflected female perceptions of relationships as well as of the world. Two of the most remarkable representatives of this period are Mechthild of Magdeburg (1212–1299) and Julian of Norwich (1342–1416).

Mechthild is a figure about whose background we know very little. She never attained sainthood, and her great book, *The Flowing Light of the Godhead,* was not made part of the "canon" of mystical classics (some of her contemporaries thought it should be burned instead). What we can piece together from her writings is that at the age of about twenty-three Mechthild decided to leave her family, friends, and small village in order to travel to the city of Magdeburg (in Germany) for a more spiritual life. She did not enter a convent. At that time convents were anything but spiritual places and were often used to house illegitimate children, unmarriageable women, even political prisoners. At some point after arriving in Magdeburg, however, Mechthild associated herself with the Beguines, a loosely organized and surprisingly open community of Christian women who led strict religious lives.

Mechthild conveys the spiritual process through images that are strange and sometimes troubling to modern readers. Most of us today tend to think of the spiritual quest as an activity that is essentially under our control, something we can choose either to pursue or not pursue, depending on our interests, inclinations, and characters. Mechthild argues just the opposite. It is not we who search for God, but God who pursues us. For modern people accustomed to viewing our lives as free and directed largely by our own efforts and choices, the thought that one of life's most powerful and transformative aspects is completely out of our hands is not very reassuring. But Mechthild goes a step further. She describes the dynamic between God and human beings as a kind of hunt, where God is the hunter and we are the hunted.

"I chased you, for in this was my pleasure," Mechthild writes, speaking in God's voice to herself. "I captured you, for this was my desire; I bound you, and I rejoice in your bonds; I have wounded you, that you may be united with me." This is a far cry from the spirituality and the spiritual language that most of us are used to these days. God does not hide, but seeks. God does not console, but wounds. The imagery of the hunt is disturbing. It matters little whether or not we choose to look for God. It does not even matter if we try to run away when God looks for us. Escape is impossible. God will find us if that is God's wish. Though the end result of this hunt may be unification with the divine, the precursor to that mystical unity is fear—fear of our own weakness, fear of that which we cannot resist.

Mechthild inverts the quest for God. It is not for us to say that we will or will not reach for the spiritual world. It will reach for us. There is no point in fighting. Our task is simply to prepare ourselves for the possibility of that moment, to brace ourselves for the collision between the Infinite and the finite. What we fear, what we experience as a brutal hunt, is from God's perspective merely an expression of divine love, a way of connecting to us at our deepest level. To submit to that love, as it is with all love, is to surrender control, to make ourselves vulnerable. Mechthild writes elsewhere that the brush with God "has such power that it takes all strength from the body and lays the soul bare to itself." Our submission to the power and presence of God can feel like an invasion. The true source of that uneasiness is not divine brutality. It is our inner encounter with the nakedness of our own souls.

Making ourselves vulnerable also means opening ourselves up to pain. When the all-powerful hunter catches up with the now powerless hunted, we are inevitably wounded. God, personified as Love, speaks again to (and through) Mechthild: "I cause you extreme pain of body. The higher the love the greater the pain." Self-surrender, even though it is the highest form of love, is extremely difficult for human beings to achieve, and it can be torturous to fully give ourselves over to another. The ecstasy (literally "out of stasis") of mystical union is disorienting and stressful. In the end, however, God makes it clear that the motivation for this meeting, despite its attendant pain, is love: "If I gave you blows, it was that you might possess me." God must sometimes kick down the doors that shield our souls in order to enter into our lives.

The biblical image of God as a consuming fire resurfaces in much of mystical literature. Mechthild, and others like her, saw God as a divine fire that filled the world. The purified souls of those who have passed their "trial by fire" are the sparks within it, united yet still distinct. Mechthild writes, "Lie down in the Fire, see and taste the flowing Godhead through your being." This fire imagery has served as a particularly precise and evocative symbol of spiritual merger, a state that, as William James notes in *The Varieties of Religious Experience,* defies linguistic expression. Still, in her writings Mechthild tries to convey to us not only her own mystical experiences, but a way that God interacts with the world. It is a vision that is unusual and often disconcerting. At times it is even frightening. But it remains a view from the edge that we must confront.

Julian of Norwich was the first woman to write a book in English. Although she gave it no name, it has been handed down to us as *A Book of Showings to the Anchoress Julian of Norwich.* It appears in two versions: the "Short Text," which consists of her initial account of a series of mystical encounters she experienced over a twenty-four-hour period in 1373; and the "Long Text," her expanded interpretation of those same events twenty years later. Julian was an anchoress, a member of a religious vocation that believed in a withdrawal from the world that was far more radical and complete than even the cloistered nuns of her era had made. While early Christian anchorites withdrew to the desert in order to pray and reflect without worldly distractions, the anchorites and anchoresses of Julian's time congregated in urban or semiurban areas. Yet they retained their calling toward the margins, living in isolated cells built against the walls of churches. Through one small window (or "squint") in her cell, an anchoress could watch worship services. Through another she could counsel visitors in the outside world.

Such extreme conditions must have surely colored Julian's spiritual outlook and writing. Her tomblike enclosure must have intensified her undistracted focus on God and prayer but also exacerbated her feelings of emotional isolation. In the *Showings,* God speaks to Julian, saying, "My darling, I am glad that thou art come to Me, in all thy woe I have ever been with thee." This association of the divine presence with woe and pain is, as we have seen, not an unfamiliar one in certain types of mysticism. God does not promise Julian a life free from hardship. What God does promise her is that when pain is present, God too will be present, even if she is not aware of it. But is that pain the result of human life or of divine love?

Though Julian's body is encased in her cell, her soul is immersed in God. "And the bodily sight stinted," she writes, trying to explain her experience, "but the spiritual sight dwelled in mine understanding, and I abode with reverent dread joying in that I saw." At the point where our physical capacities end, our spiritual vitality can take over. Mystical insight—the deeper vision of our souls—can surpass the limitations of the senses. If there is discomfort or fear, they are mingled with love and joy. It is harrowing to transcend the straits of the body, to witness the crumbling of the self. God's embrace can hurt, even if it does lead us to spiritual union. The mystic way is not always a path of peace.

Our achievement of union with God is not a unilateral ambition, but the realization of a mutual desire. God wants us as much as we want God. Despite the fear and pain that can be connected to our brush with divinity, humanity and God share an innate yearning for each other. "For our natural Will," Julian writes, "is to have God, and the Good will of God is to have us." A kind of spiritual hunger, even lust, pervades the universe. Like Adam and Eve, or two partners in a marriage, humanity is incomplete until we have made God a fundamental part of our lives and souls, and God is incomplete until God has done the same. Hunger is not a pleasant feeling, and it is a condition that most of us do not want to live with. But it can impel us toward God in ways nothing else can, especially when we know that the ultimate encounter will be jarring and difficult.

The drive may be the same, but the relationship between God and humanity is not one of equality. We saw how Mechthild described the dynamic in terms of the hunter and the hunted. Julian's description is even more unsettling: God is the predator and we are the prey. "And we shall endlessly be all had in God," she writes of the experience of mystical union, "Him verily seeing and fully feeling, Him spiritually hearing and Him delectably smelling and sweetly swallowing." Julian describes a God who sees, feels, hears, smells, and *eats.* Like the Torah's image of God as a consuming fire, Julian's vision portrays God as a ravenous being who "swallows" all of humanity during the rapture of spiritual union. This vision of eternity—or at least the brief glimpse of it we can sometimes have—is sensual and stark. It is also fairly disturbing. God is portrayed almost as a kind of animal, intent on preying on our souls so as to satiate the divine appetite. The result may be ecstasy, but the process is feasting.

The goal of the mystic is the direct encounter with God. As Mechthild of Magdeburg and Julian of Norwich make clear, however, this lofty and transformative event, this "dark rapture," is not easy to achieve. Or to endure. Before mystical union can occur, we must first stare fear in the face. We must make ourselves vulnerable. And from the vantage points of these two women mystics, we must lose ourselves and allow God to ravage us, like a wild but caring lover. These are not images of spirituality or of God that most of us are familiar with, yet the themes and concepts behind them are not exclusively feminine, or even exclusively Christian. Several centuries later a Jewish mystic expressed similar views.

When he was a young man, before he became one of the greatest hasidic masters of his time, Rabbi Dov Baer of Mezeritch (who died in 1772) was an ascetic. Like other religious ascetics, Dov Baer would often spend his days and weeks fasting, praying, and in contemplation. His regimen was severe, and his spiritual practices frequently left him exhausted and ill. Legend has it that after one particularly grave illness that nearly cost him his life, Dov Baer made a pilgrimage to the town of Miedzyboz in the Ukraine to seek out the Baal Shem Tov, the "Master of the Good Name" and charismatic founder of Hasidism, whose renown as a healer and teacher was widespread throughout the lands in which the Jews of eastern Europe then lived.

This brush with death, coupled with his encounter with the Baal Shem Tov, seems to have changed Dov Baer's life. Hasidism, as taught by its founder, rejected asceticism and other expressions of self-negation as appropriate ways of serving God. Instead it advocated a spirituality rooted in joy and pleasure, viewing even the most mundane of human acts (like eating, drinking, and sex) as vehicles for celebrating life and worshipping its Creator. Dov Baer abandoned his earlier form of spirituality and embraced this radical movement, soon becoming a key figure in the Baal Shem Tov's inner circle of disciples. It was Dov Baer, known now as the Great Maggid (preacher), who eventually became the successor of the Baal Shem Tov and the new leader of Hasidism after his master's death in 1760.

Despite his abandonment of asceticism, those darker impulses that had originally propelled him toward Hasidism survived his conversion. Unlike the skill of the Baal Shem Tov, who was able to popularize hasidic teachings, the Maggid's talent lay—in large part because of his extensive education—in his ability to influence scholars, whether Kabbalists or mainstream rabbis. His writings are expansive and profound, but in them we find a man still very much at the edge, a man who has managed to sublimate his physio-spiritual impulses toward self-denial and self-denigration into a contemplative form of mysticism imbued with the idea that our relationship with God is not always one that is marked by pleasure and comfort. The Maggid offers a much darker, though equally spiritual, vision of Hasidism than that of his mentor.

One of the key motifs in the Maggid's mystical writings is that of fear. Like Mechthild and Julian, the Maggid presents us with a description of mystical union with God that is at times disconcerting.

For him, one of the principal ways a person can reach the spiritual summit of *devekut* ("adhesion" with God) is through the experience not of joy, but of fear. The Maggid describes two fundamental categories of religious fear: the fear of punishment (the lower order of fear) and the fear of God's majesty (the higher order). It is the first type of fear, which relates to our awareness of our moral failings, that is the first rung on the ladder of spiritual development. If we do not even fear that our wrongdoings have necessary consequences—which implies the existence of a Judge who rewards and punishes—our relationships with God will be stunted. The fear of punishment is the acceptance of divine sovereignty. Morality is the stepping-stone to spirituality.

Yet neither ethics nor knowledge alone will lead us to God. For that we need to stir up the spiritual embers that smolder within us. Fear can achieve that. There is a story about the first meeting between the Maggid and the Baal Shem Tov. At midnight, as Dov Baer waited in an inn for his audience with the great master, a messenger arrived. He was to come at once. The Baal Shem Tov was waiting. When Dov Baer entered the master's chamber, he was asked if he was well versed in the Kabbalah. Dov Baer said that he was. The Baal Shem Tov then handed him a holy book and asked him to expound on a passage that dealt with angels. He did so brilliantly. "You have no true knowledge," the master said, ordering the shaken Dov Baer to rise. The Baal Shem Tov proceeded to recite the same passage. Suddenly, before Dov Baer's eyes, the room was engulfed by flames, and through the blaze he heard the singing of angels until he lost consciousness. When he awoke, the room was as it had been when he entered it. The Baal Shem Tov stood opposite him and said: "You expounded correctly, but you lack true understanding, for there is no soul in what you know."

It is not rational analysis, but spiritual vitality that unlocks the gates of religious insight, that connects human beings to God. The young Rabbi Baer did not fear the Baal Shem Tov. What he feared, what overwhelmed him, was the force of the spirituality that his master was able to summon from within himself. For all of his academic training and intellectual knowledge, Dov Baer could not yet gain access to his own soul. But it was this awesome encounter, and the experience of confronting his own deficiencies, that would catalyze his inner quest and lead to his many years of spiritual apprenticeship with the Baal Shem Tov.

Once our baser fears have awakened us to the reality of the transcendent, we become far more receptive to the second, higher form of religious fear, the fear of God's majesty. The Maggid uses an analogy, as he does in much of his writing, to convey this message: "The most lofty level of fear," he writes, "is when a subject fears his king out of shame, for the king is great and awe-inspiring. Because of this, the subject loves him even more, for though the king is powerful and awesome, he still watches over and satisfies the needs of all the subjects in his kingdom." In this parable on the relationship between humanity and God, the subject fears his king not because he anticipates harm or punishment from him (the lower type of fear), but out of reverence and awe in the face of his benefactor. The shame the subject feels has as much to do with the king's majesty as it does with the subject's own sense of worth. In this dynamic, fear, shame, and love all coalesce into a single totality.

After one has managed to attain this level of spiritual elevation, the next step is *devekut,* union with God. It is here where the Maggid's ascetic impulses begin to resurface even more clearly. Explicating the verse "What does the Lord your God require of you, but to fear the Lord your God?" (Deut. 10:12), he writes that "one must vigorously engage in the contemplation of God's greatness and majesty until one arrives at the level of nothingness," a state brought about through the experiences of fear and shame. "Nothingness," in the mystical context, is the collapse of self-consciousness, the disintegration of individual identity that results from a brush with divinity.

Fear is the medium that leads to and accompanies self-negation. The Maggid compares the process of mystical absorption to a candle placed before a torch: just as a candle is useless and unable to function if it is too close to the torch, so are the abilities and capacities of a person (temporarily) wiped out while in the presence of God. The fear that is part of this encounter negates not only the person's other thoughts and emotions, but also his very sense of self. Fear is the cause of self-annihilation as well as the connective tissue between God and the mystic. At the moment of *devekut,* according to the Maggid, a "fire of silence" descends upon the mystic and a "great fear" grips his soul. He cannot see or hear. He no longer knows where he is or even who he is. In this state of ecstasy, the border between the material and the spiritual dimensions blurs. This is the edge, the void through which God is able to enter into his life. Mystical death becomes the precursor to a revitalized life.

The Maggid's thought, as well as his life, was clearly influenced by the teachings of the Baal Shem Tov. Inner spirituality, as opposed to external factors such as ascetic practice or religious study, is treated as the foundation of a life with God. But that is where the similarity ends. At its core, the Maggid's spirituality is not one that is rooted in joy and celebration. It is marked instead by notions of fear, shame, and self-negation. His asceticism has not disappeared. It has been transposed onto his mysticism. This tension appears throughout the Maggid's writing. Despite his best efforts to embrace the inherent optimism of early Hasidism, his attraction to the darker side of spirituality remained with him for the rest of his life.

The Maggid's elevated sense of spirituality and self-transcendence left a deep impression on his many disciples. For twelve years he led the nascent hasidic movement, choosing the best of his students to become the leaders of hasidic communities throughout Poland and

Russia and inspiring the less sophisticated audiences through stirring sermons and homilies. Despite this, the rabbinic authorities of the time saw the Hasidim as "destroyers of Israel" because of what they viewed as their radical, even heretical, teachings. In the spring of 1772 several towns banned hasidic congregations from meeting and had their members excommunicated. When news of these bans reached the aged Maggid, along with reports of other persecutions against members of his mystical movement (including some of his own disciples), he fell ill and soon died. How much of this was due to a broken heart as well we will never know.

Fear can link us to the spiritual world in ways that are not always obvious. In the first book of Kings, the Israelite prophet Elijah lashes out at the idolatrous prophets of Baal, an eruption of zealous rage that drives him to kill. In the shadow of Mount Carmel he slaughters all 450 of them by the sword. When his anger cools and his senses return, he realizes what he has done. He is in enemy territory and flees for his life. It is fear, the fear of death, that sends him into the desert wilderness and unknowingly toward a brush with God. Stripped of his earlier cockiness and posturing ("I am no better than my fathers," he now admits), brought face-to-face with his own vulnerability, he becomes attuned to the nuances of authentic spirituality. Elijah encounters God, not through the raptures of religious warfare or nature's spectacular displays of wind, earthquakes, and fire, but in "a still small voice." (19:12)

That voice can sometimes become a roar. Our awareness of the chasm that separates humanity from God does not always lead to reverence or awe. It can result in terror. That experience can strike any of us, not just mystics. At perhaps the most profound spiritual moment in human history, as God appears on Mount Sinai and reveals the Ten Commandments to the Israelites, the chosen people (all six hundred thousand of them) are gripped with fear and trembling: "On the third day, as morning dawned, there was thunder, and lightning, and a dense cloud upon the mountain, and a very loud blast of the horn. And all the people who were in the camp trembled." (Exodus 19:16) Moses leads his people to the foot of the mountain, where they prepare for the revelation in silence.

Mount Sinai is covered in smoke, for "the Lord had come down upon it in fire." (19:18) As the smoke rises toward heaven "like the smoke of a kiln," the mountain itself begins to tremble as a consequence of God's presence. The blast of the horn grows louder and louder: it sounds like the shrieking of a wild animal. God descends to the top of the mountain and tells Moses to warn the Israelites not to draw too close, not to look through the smoke and clouds and try to gaze at God's essence. Even the priests are ordered to stand at a distance. When the people witness the thunder and lightning and hear the words of God, they fall back and retreat to an even greater distance from the mountain. "You speak to us," they implore Moses, "let not God speak to us, lest we die." (20:16) Moses answers them with what appears to be a contradiction. He tells them not to be afraid, that God has become manifest only to test their obedience, that they will survive this encounter. But Moses also tells them that the very purpose of the theophany at Sinai was to instill in them a sense of fear, "that the fear of Him may be ever with you." (20:17)

From the perspective of humanity, God is the great Other, the ungraspable mystery hidden by smoke. The unmediated, tangible presence of God in our lives can seem as elusive to us today as it did to the Israelites thousands of years before. Yet our desire to see God is, at its heart, only a mask for our wanting to be God—an aspiration as dangerous as it is impossible. Some knowledge is forbidden. Our vision of the divine must remain clouded and couched in fear. In the spiritual context, even at those times that we stand at the frontiers of human experience, fear is our protection, the religious equivalent of the blood that the Israelite slaves brushed on their doorposts to guard themselves against the angel of death. It is our way of respecting the boundary that must forever separate the created from their Creator, the finite from the Infinite. There may be moments in our lives when that boundary breaks down, when we get a temporary glimpse of God's presence. That glimpse can change our lives, but, like a flame before a torch, we must return to a safe distance if we are to regain our sense of self and prevent our being devoured permanently by the divine fire.

The spiritual experiences of most of us are usually far less dramatic than those had by the mystics. But fear can still play an important role in our inner lives. Whether we fear bears, commitments, or death, that fear is only the outer garment for something deeper within it. Maybe even something holy. In *Moby-Dick* Ahab says, "All visible objects, man, are but as pasteboard masks" for the truer objects that lurk hidden behind their surfaces. Our challenge is to strip away those masks, those outer veils, that separate us from—yet, paradoxically, connect us to—the higher spiritual realities.

Although there are an unlimited number of fears a human being can experience during his or her lifetime, all of them share a single but invisible root: the fear of God. Whatever we may think we fear, the real source of our dread and anxiety is ultimately our own humanity, our inability to control our destinies, our finitude in the face of God's infinity. A spirituality that utilizes fear as a springboard for inner growth is not about succumbing to it, but about seeing through it. If we are ready, if we are spiritually mature, this insight should lead not to despair, but to liberation and enlightenment. As the Bible clearly states, "The fear of the Lord is the beginning of wisdom." (Psalms 111:10)

4 / inward bound

The very meaning of the ascetic ideal is this: that there was something missing, that an immense void surrounded man;—he did not know how to justify, explain, affirm himself; he suffered from the problem of his being. . . . Man, the bravest and most long-suffering beast, does not deny suffering in itself; he wants it, he even searches it out, provided a meaning for it be shown him, a "what for" of his suffering. The senselessness of suffering, not suffering, was the curse that had hitherto been lying upon man;—and the ascetic ideal provided a meaning.

FRIEDRICH NIETZSCHE, *On the Genealogy of Morals*

The road that began for me in Los Angeles unraveled ahead over sagebrush and sand. I was listening to a Hank Williams song, "The Lost Highway," as I drove past the border into Nevada: *I'm a rolling stone, all alone and low. . . .*

I'd been driving for only a short time, and I still had a country to cross—the Rockies, the badlands, the plains—before I would make a brief stop at my parents' home in Chicago. My second year of the seminary had just ended. I was moving out to New York City to continue my rabbinical studies, and I had orders to report to Fort Monmouth, New Jersey, in two weeks to begin basic training as an army chaplain. There was a lot to think about. Yet all I could do was think of her. Like the twenty-two-year-old in the song, I had fallen for a woman who'd captured my heart and then left me twisting in the wind, aimless, beyond hope or even prayer.

I was lost. Not according to the map, but in my soul. I wasn't sure whether Hank's droning voice was a source of comfort or numbness, but somehow his ruminations on love and loss seemed to connect with my inmost feelings. Stories about the loss of first loves are nothing new, of course, and I had heard plenty of them in the past. What most of those stories failed to convey, however, was just how stunning and disorienting such experiences could be to a young man. I needed to experience that loss myself before I could truly understand its pain.

When my girlfriend was in my life, I felt that I had found the three things I most craved: meaning, a sense of wholeness, and rest. I wanted more and more to shake off the continued Sturm und Drang of my mid-twenties, but my soul was still at war with itself. I knew I was going to be a rabbi, but I'd be goddamned, I told myself, if I would let that stop me from sucking the marrow out of life while I was young and able. That hunger had driven me to some unusual places, from a prison cell to the wilds of Alaska. Yet it was becoming ever clearer to me that my storm was in need of an eye.

I met her in Jerusalem after a poetry reading. She had taken the year off from Princeton University to play the French horn with the city's symphony, and she was only nineteen. I had seen her before at a gathering or two earlier in the semester (I was in my first year of rabbinical school at the time), but I figured she was too young for me—even though I was only twenty-four myself. She approached me after the reading to tell me how much she liked my poem, and we began a conversation. I was taken by her forthrightness, and I used it as my license to ask her out on a date. Two months later, when she told me she loved me, my world was transformed.

There are few things as powerful—or as transient—as a Jerusalem romance. The sunsets dust the Temple Mount with copper and gold. The mingling of ancient stones with modern steel makes time seem to dissolve, leaving a strange sort of residue that cups every tower and coats every street. (In grimmer moments such spiritual weight can feel oppressive, as if the whole city sits on the verge of implosion.) It was in this highly charged atmosphere that the two of us fell in love, and it was this love that I carried back with me when the academic year ended and my girlfriend and I had to return to the States, each of us to a different coast.

We continued our relationship from long distance. I had never been in love before, not even close to it. For the first time I had let another person deep into my heart, and I began to feel a kind of rootedness that at times, owing to my own history of dis-ease with that organ and with all the constraints and weaknesses it represented, felt almost imprisoning. That year in Los Angeles was the worst year of my life. Because I was riveted by this new experience of love, the rest of my world deadened. I lived a shadow life, cloistered in my apartment and venturing out only to go to classes or an occasional film. All I could do was think of my girlfriend—and lament that she was so far away. I thought that this was how love was supposed to be. My girlfriend the human being (young, beautiful, talented) and my girlfriend the idea (purpose, completeness, peace) merged into a single reality. Blind to the fact that in either case I had objectified her, and ignoring my unhappiness, I made her the center of my universe.

My seminary had a vacation period during Passover, and I planned to spend the full week with my girlfriend at Princeton. Prior to that, the two of us had spent only three long weekends together. Except for the few months in Jerusalem, our relationship had evolved over the phone. We knew each other far less than we assumed. I knew that she loved me, but I didn't really know *her,* or the questions that she might have been asking herself about our relationship. Looking back on it, I realize she might very well have been objectifying me too, turning me into the dark and tormented soul that would stir up her staid and stuffy world of fencing and eating clubs.

I sensed there was a problem from the moment I arrived on campus. My girlfriend seemed strangely distant, and we barely touched each other that first night. (She said she was tired.) While she went to her classes the next day, I stayed in her room. Her bed was so small that when I visited her we would have to pull off her two mattresses from the box spring and sleep on the floor. I spent the entire morning and afternoon on my back, staring at the ceiling. I knew what was coming. I just couldn't believe it was actually happening. How could God hand me the gift of love and then snatch it away? How could God center me and then pull the rug out from under my feet? I started to cry. Then I began to pray.

"Please, God," I said aloud, "don't let this end." I reviewed the past year in my mind. My life in Los Angeles was a nightmare, of that I was certain, but it couldn't have been the fault of the relationship with my girlfriend. I was always so happy when she was in my arms. . . . Soon it became clear to me that I was praying the prayer of a child, pleading for a toy that was being taken away from me. I did not want that to be the sort of prayer I had on my lips, the lips of a future rabbi. "Show me the way," I whispered. But I wasn't sure if I really wanted to see it.

My girlfriend returned to her room near dusk. "We need to talk," she said. We walked on the golf course behind her dorm, found a large sand trap, and sat down. I was seeing a woman I had never seen before, hard, shut down. She told me of the longtime doubts she had harbored about the two of us, the ways in which we were radically different kinds of people. "I'm so young," she cried. "I have so much more of life I need to experience before I can be in something this heavy. I don't even know who I am yet." A hole opened up inside me, a fresh one, smack in the center of my rib cage.

Everything suddenly became surreal. As we walked slowly back to her room, a group of deer darted across the grass in front of us and into the woods. The scene was beautiful, but I was numb. The core had collapsed. My girlfriend was becoming a ghost before my eyes. She was leaving my world, and leaving me to the struggle from which I had tried so hard to escape. Only twenty-four hours into my visit, I packed my clothes, hugged her, and said good-bye. I wasn't sure what to do or where to go. I stood alone on the platform at Princeton Junction. There was nothing within me but the sensation of loss. A light appeared out of the darkness. It was the train to New York. I had friends there. Maybe they would take me in.

As the train drew closer, I shuffled over to the edge of the platform. I watched as the train roared into the station. I looked down at the tracks. I hesitated. Then I backed away from the edge.

I had created a dream world, a stage set—not really fake, not exactly real, but *imagined.* When that creation was taken away, I was lost. The things that had helped to center me before I had met my now ex-girlfriend had been eclipsed by her, and I found it almost impossible to retrieve them. When I returned to Los Angeles, the religious rituals that had once inspired me felt burdensome and pointless. Praying became more and more difficult. The thoughts and emotions that had directed my life had been wrested from me, and I didn't know how to respond. I couldn't hate her (which would have eventually pushed out the painful feelings of longing from my soul), and I didn't want to live with the sorrow and confusion that had taken her place. The loss of a first love was bad enough, but I was training to become a rabbi, a religious leader; my grief was starting to turn me away from religion itself. I knew I had to do something. To mark the loss and work through it. To regain my spiritual bearings.

Toward the middle of the summer I went into the White Mountains of New Hampshire. I brought a rain tarp, my sleeping bag, and a journal. No food or books, not even a watch. Nothing to link me to the outside world. The plan, based on the Native American vision quest (but with a decidedly Jewish twist), was to spend three days and nights seeking insight and healing alone in the wilderness, without food, shelter, or human contact. I had fasted on the Day of Atonement for years, so I had some idea of what hunger tasted like. The fasting didn't intimidate me. It was the uncertainty about what I would find within.

Making a journey—especially a journey into the inner wilderness—can be difficult. And sometimes frightening. We are not certain how long it will take us to reach our destination. We don't know what kinds of obstacles we might confront along the way. We are not always sure what we will find at the end of the path. Or if we will reach an end at all. For some of us, this uncertainty can create such anxiety that we become too scared even to take the first step. We get paralyzed by our own souls. It was at this point, when I began to feel frozen by my own broken heart, that I knew I had to get to the mountains, that I had to put myself through a physical ordeal in order to make sense of my pain and revitalize the life of my spirit.

I searched my map for a region as removed as possible from the more visited spots off Route 93, places with names like the Flume, the Basin, and Franconia Notch. I settled on the Pemigewasset Wilderness, an area dead in the center of the forest. After parking my car at a trailhead, I hiked in about six miles to the edge of a cluster of jagged, exposed peaks called the Cliffs. I didn't want to hike in any deeper because I was alone and I figured that three days without food would take their toll on my return.

There was no flat ground anywhere, so I placed my tarp over a small, stony clearing just off the trail. Dark, thick trees—and mosquitoes that grew thicker by the minute from my blood—were my only companions. Suddenly it started to rain. Hard. I had been there less than half an hour and already I had a problem. With nothing but a green tarp to keep me dry, I rolled it like a tobacco leaf around my body and backpack. I waited. The rain pelted the plastic with a rhythm that was almost hypnotic. I started to doze, and as I did I noticed that inches above my head was a fly, upside down, motionless, and safe beneath a leaf of its own.

Odd things occurred. I had fallen into a state in which I couldn't tell if I were asleep or awake. I think I was both at the same time. I heard sounds. The patter of paws. Steps. I felt encircled by other beings. Watched by them. Dreams and reality became porous, intermingling at will. I didn't feel alone. Nor did I feel secure. And when the rain ended and I emerged from my cocoon, unsure of how long or even whether I had been asleep, I grew anxious about making a journey into the wilderness of my soul. I had turned my girlfriend into my ticket to inner peace, and now she was gone. But she was wrong for me, and, though I couldn't admit that truth while we were together, I had always sensed it deep inside. I could no longer proceed in a straight line because the straight line itself had become the line of error. I knew I had to diverge from that trail and trudge in the dark through the muck and mire if I wanted to move on.

We don't always know where our journeys will lead us. Often we just have to wander. I had no clue what my life would look like with my girlfriend no longer in it. Roaming alone through the White Mountains seemed like as good a way as any to place myself at the mercy of my future. It was also a good way to cope with tedium. The hardest part of my vision quest, it turned out, wasn't the fasting; after the first twenty-four hours I wasn't really hungry at all. It was the boredom. And the burden of being with no one but myself. With an exploded sense of time (my only real tool for measuring it was the position of the sun), and without the ritual of meals or meetings, I learned quickly about the deep and sometimes desperate human need for structure.

In order to fend off the boredom and forget the fact of my solitude, I created structure for myself. (Though I had brought with me a pair of tefillin, or phylacteries, so I could feel there was at least some Jewish content to the vision quest, I was too despondent to make myself utilize the structures and rituals of my faith.) I took hikes. I wrote poetry. I did anything I could to avoid being with myself. Yet when dusk arrived and even writing in my journal became an impossibility, I had no other choice but to acknowledge myself. I was alone. But I was alive. I had entered the borderland, the frontier that separated my past from my future. Nothing since has been as silent as that first night in the woods. It was a silence as swollen with life as the darkness around me.

On my last day I decided to visit the Cliffs, a three-hour hike in each direction. The minute I stepped onto the trail I started to cry. I was not quite certain what triggered the tears, nor was I completely sure of what kind of tears they were. Tears of loss, that much I could figure out. But they were also tears of acknowledgment. As if the wilderness were affirming my finitude, telling me that the pain of being human was not something that was always negative. If I put it in its proper context, that pain could even help me. With this knowledge that my past would not cripple me and that the future was beyond my power to control, I began the ascent.

I walked along a brook for much of the trail. Its cool water rippled over stones and branches; miniature frogs hunched motionless on either bank. The higher I hiked, the more stunted the trees became, until they soon disappeared altogether. On the ridge above the tree line, and then strewn all over the cliffs themselves, were rock cairns, traces of those souls who had been to the summit before me. Birds bathed in pools from the recent rains. One dashed up to me and defecated.

The cliffs were barren, and the winds that gusted over them chilled me. From that vantage point I had a 360-degree view of the region; it looked like a great green blanket, and if I hadn't known that within it were trails and roads, I'd have doubted that human civilization had ever touched it. The clouds rolled over the cliffs in caricatures, the sun pressing their shadows into the soil below. Two hawks soared past me. Then two more. Soon I saw half a dozen of them, leaping from ledge to ledge, gliding with the updrafts into the sky. There seemed to be no purpose to their play. I sat on a boulder and watched them for what must have been hours. I couldn't move. I was too much at peace.

I made it back to my tarp just as the dusk began to set in. The woods darkened. I took out a candle from my backpack and stuck it in the ground. I wanted to burn off the residue of a romanticized past and light the way toward an unclear future. For three days I had let hunger and solitude reshape my soul. I knew my relationship with my ex-girlfriend had been riddled with problems. What I had lacked was the inner strength to move ahead. I needed the help of outside forces in order to transcend regret and self-pity, to get on with the task of living my life and expanding my spirit. I had done nothing in the White Mountains *but* live—no interactions, no work, no rigid regimentation. That was what made it so difficult. I had stripped myself bare and stared into the face of my own humanity, my own suffering. Now I felt ready to return to the world, to the routines and rituals that in my sadness had seemed so meaningless. I was prepared to accept my future and embrace yet more uncertainty. I lit the candle. And I remembered the words of Rabbi Menahem Mendel of Kotsk, who observed, "There is nothing more whole than a broken heart."

The morning was cold. Yet for the first time in weeks the first words out of my mouth formed a prayer: *Elohai, neshamah shenatatah bi tehorah hi*—"My God, the soul you have given me is a pure one." Fasting in the wilderness had cleansed me. I took out my tefillin, an old, beaten pair that had once belonged to my grandfather and that had been given to me shortly after his death two years before. I wrapped the cracked leather straps around my left biceps and adjusted the headpiece over my forehead. It felt as if I were being held in my grandfather's arms. I said the morning prayers. And I wondered: Was I over her? *Really* over her? I doubted it. But I could pray again. I could at least do that.

Asceticism has played a constant role in the history of world religions. Yet many of us today view it negatively, understanding the phenomenon as a pathology of self-hatred and an escape from the world. This armchair analysis sells asceticism short. The ascetic impulse can be found, in varying degrees and through diverse forms, in most spiritual traditions. Some of its common manifestations include fasting, isolation, flight to the wilderness, sexual abstinence, denial of certain foods, and self-mortification. In comparison with other ascetic practices, my vision quest, though effective as a vehicle for personal growth, was rather mild. The underlying motivation for all of these rituals, however, is a uniform one. Asceticism is our response to a tension that inheres in all religious systems: the drive of human beings (either as individuals or as groups) to achieve an ideal of spiritual perfection while simultaneously confronting a self and a world that perpetually undermine that quest.

An ascetic tries to overcome those barriers. One model is the Nazir, a member of an entire class of ascetics that lived in biblical and Second Temple times. What separated these men from other Israelites was their devotion, for a given period, to specific disciplines (delineated in chapter 6 of the book of Numbers) intended to promote ritual and spiritual purity: abstention from wine and other grape products; avoidance of contact with the dead; refusal to cut their hair; and vowing to set their lives apart from their community in order to serve God exclusively. Since these behaviors are all visible, public ones, many rabbis came to view the Nazir with a degree of suspicion, concerned that the motivation of some of them had more to do with vanity and getting noticed than with the sincere desire to control or channel their impulse toward sin.

One of the most famous (and tragic) examples of the Nazir is Samson, the great warrior-hero from the book of Judges. His Nazirite/ascetic practices result in an infusion of the "spirit of God" into his soul, an infusion that leads to extraordinary prowess in his battles with the Philistines and other enemies. Yet the metaphysical power unleashed by Samson's asceticism ultimately consumes him. Later, betrayed by the woman he loves and captured by his tormentors, he utters a death wish: "Let me die with the Philistines." (16:30) The blind and bound Samson then pulls down the pillars of their temple and crushes everyone inside it, including himself. It is an act of vengeance and rage, and it shows how the same rituals of abstinence that can give us inner strength and direct us toward self-improvement can, depending on our psychological dispositions, also drive us to self-destruction.

Another model of Jewish asceticism was the Essene community, an enigmatic and secretive group that lived during the intertestamental period (about 200 B.C.E. to 100 C.E.) in a remote area of the land of Israel known as Qumran. There, in the solitude of the desert and in the cliffs above the Dead Sea, these individuals wrote what have come to be known as the Dead Sea Scrolls. The Essenes were sectarians, having broken away (many scholars think) from the priesthood in Jerusalem, which they believed had been corrupted by sin. For them, even the Temple itself had fallen prey to evil forces. They viewed themselves as God's vanguard, the "sons of light" who would soon wage war against the powers of darkness and return the world to the rule of God. Their messianism was rooted in asceticism, in a disciplined way of life that was intended to whip them into spiritual shape for the great apocalyptic battle to come.

In the Essene worldview, discipline and suffering were thought to have atoning power, both for themselves and for all of Israel. In order to defeat the forces of darkness, God's warriors had to be pure. Abstinence was a crucial component in their spiritual training program. Unlike the pietistic practices of other Jewish groups at the time, celibacy played an important role in the religious life of the Essene community. Sexual desire, as well as the bonds of marriage, were viewed by most of them as impediments to their solitary task: preparation for Doomsday. Piety, study, and communal solidarity were the focal points of their lives. Anything that lured them away from these activities had to be avoided at all costs. Yet the Dead Sea Scrolls seem to assume the existence of women and even cases of marriage within the semimonastic order and do not speak of permanent celibacy. What this suggests is that the Essenes were a more complex and diverse community than the usual portrayal of them implies, still holding on (tenuously) to the Jewish obligation to procreate. Although their asceticism drove them, both geographically and theologically, to the far reaches of the Jewish world, it was as Jews that they wanted to face Armageddon, an Armageddon that never arrived.

When the Romans sacked Jerusalem in 70 C.E., in addition to slaughtering many thousands of innocent people and destroying the Second Temple, they also wiped out a religious system that had supported the Jewish people for centuries. In the aftermath of this tragedy there was an eruption of asceticism, as Jews turned inward in an attempt to cope with their suffering and loss. It was most likely one of the few spiritual mechanisms that helped many of them through this painful period of transition. A millennium later, the ravages of the Crusades left profound scars on the psyche of medieval

German Jewry. Not surprisingly, a new movement in Jewish asceticism, led by the German Pietists (or *Hasidei Ashkenaz*), emerged on the religious scene as yet another generation of Jews struggled to find meaning in light of human suffering.

Most of what we know about the Pietists comes from the writings of their two most prominent figures, Judah the Pious (about 1150–1217) and his disciple, Eleazar of Worms (who died in 1230). Although the particular focus of the two rabbis was different (Judah was concerned with the spiritual life of the Jewish community, while Eleazar's interest was more in the soul of the individual Jew), both of them shared a vision of the pietistic ideal: A true Hasid had to wholeheartedly strive to discover, and then perform, the hidden will of God. The three elements that were critical to this task were the renunciation of the material world, serenity of mind, and extreme altruism. Since God's will was only partially revealed through the Torah, the Pietist had to go *beyond* the requirements of Jewish law, creating "extra" prohibitions and obligations for himself. Yet this spiritual mission would be impeded not only by our own limitations and weaknesses, but by the trials and obstacles that God places in our path in order to strengthen us.

The Pietists interpreted the rabbinic maxim "You shall be forever resourceful in fearing God" as a justification for their ascetic system. Fear of God was, for them, the radical, selfless dedication to serve God out of love. To be "resourceful" was to grasp as yet unknown prohibitions and practices and then to perform them. "Fear" was the governing force, but only proper fear would lead to true and pure dedication. Fear of the threat of future punishment was selfish. Fear based on not losing one's petitionary power in prayer was also self-serving. Only fear of not being perfect before God, of falling short of loving God for its own sake, was selfless and acceptable.

Another maxim that the Pietists utilized was "Reward is proportional to pain." This introduced the idea of an ordeal or trial into their spirituality. To fulfill God's will is no easy task. Temporal lusts will compete against eternal truths for our souls: the human inclination to do evil must be overcome if we are to advance in our inner journeys. To the Pietists, this impulse is God's tool for testing our spiritual mettle. But it is not enough merely to avoid temptation; we must be subjected to it continuously through a series of trials. Without them there would be no opportunity to resist, no chance to demonstrate our dedication to God. Trials are gifts, not burdens. Whatever pain the Pietist experiences in his worldly task will be countered by an equal reward in the World to Come. Because Pietism is a process, not an end in itself, the divine scales of judgment are central to it. The double benefit of a trial is that it allows the Pietist to follow God's will and resist the temptation to violate it at the same time.

When we sin we fail to live up to the pietistic ideal. What happens when would-be Pietists fall short (as they inevitably will) in their spiritual mission? German Pietism developed a system of penitence to safeguard against such pitfalls. The Pietists had four different categories of penitence, each related to a specific type, and degree, of sin. Confession and penance were essential parts of this structure, one which sought to correct the imbalance in the divine scales that sin caused. After formal repentance (often involving a verbal confession to a sage-confessor), the Pietist had to make a vow not to repeat the sin. But repentance is not always enough. There must sometimes be penance. In German asceticism, sins and virtuous acts do not simply "cancel out" one another. While the Bible lists penalties for particular sins, the Pietist had to *add* a penalty for the illicit pleasure he derived from the sin or for its gravity. Penance could take the form of an ice bath in mid-winter, self-flagellation, smearing one's body with honey and being stung by bees, or endless periods of fasting.

Judah the Pious, the founder of German Pietism, led a life of extreme asceticism, fasting nearly every day and eating only at night.

He was the anonymous author of many works, but his most popular and influential book was *Sefer Hasidim, The Book of the Pious.* It is comprised of case histories, teachings, and aphorisms that speak to the hearts as well as the minds of its readers. Here is a short selection:

> A man whose [sinful] inclination overpowers him is permitted to afflict himself in order to conquer it.
>
> A man should not walk arrogantly or with an uncovered head, because God's glory is above him.
>
> All meritorious actions that a man performs which do not have humility [in] them are like a meal without salt, and all humility that does not have the fear of Heaven in it is like food without spices.
>
> One should not fear [God] because of punishments in the time to come, or for the sake of enjoyment in this world or the next, but rather lest he not be perfect in his love for the Creator, may His name be blessed.
>
> If a person restrains his imagination, lowers his eyes so as not to gaze at women, does not talk banalities, suppresses his anger, does not act haughtily, engages in Torah study, and acts benevolently, in the future world he will be closer to God than the angels.

Eleazar of Worms, Judah's most zealous and important student, taught a similar form of Jewish asceticism, but with a more personalist, less communal, emphasis. During the process of atonement, for instance, Eleazar made the need for a sage-confessor obsolete. And unlike Judah, Eleazar did not write anonymously. In the introduction to his great legal and ethical code, *Sefer ha-Rokeach,* he instructs the reader as to why he is writing it: "I contemplated the world's vanities, which are false and insignificant; that this world is a passing world, and the days of man are few. I will write a book so one may race to it and find the secret matters in order to perform [God's will]." Below are some of Eleazar's teachings:

> There is no crown like humility.
> There is no enemy like lustful desire.
> Hate nothing as much as pride.
> Do not seek to know the origin of things.
> There is no love like the love of God.

For the German Pietists, proper internal attitudes and intentions were just as important as external disciplines and practices. The goal of their asceticism was spiritual perfection. The road they used to reach it was one of psychic and physical trial.

Similar, and in many cases more radical, expressions of religious asceticism began to emerge in the non-Jewish world. A few centuries after the Essenes, a group of Christian ascetics also took flight to the desert. For them, withdrawal from the ordinary ways of life in order to focus purely on spiritual matters was not enough; they separated themselves completely from the congregations and the cities of their day (fourth century) and fled deep into the deserts of Egypt, Palestine, Arabia, and Persia. These were the very first Christian hermits, who abandoned the pagan world in which they lived and sought salvation in solitude and seclusion. The Desert Fathers refused to be ruled by the decrees and mores of men, accepting only the sovereignty of God and concentrating, through blistering days and frigid nights, on how to bring their wills into alignment with the will of the Almighty.

One of the earliest of these new desert ascetics was St. Anthony. The son of rich parents who died while he was a young man, Anthony gave away all of his family's wealth to the poor and began to live an ascetic life near his home. Yet the distractions around him were still too great, and soon he felt the need to withdraw totally from society and other human beings. Anthony entered and was sealed in several caves in the desert, where, according to his ancient biographer (St. Athanasius), he survived a succession of temptations and trials by the devil. While these contests may be more legendary than factual, we can imagine the inner demons that such a worldly, affluent young man had to wrestle with while severed from the comforts of his home and entombed under the desert sun. But this father of the Desert Fathers viewed his self-imposed seclusion as the best path for gaining the freedom to pursue holiness—as well as discover his own unencumbered soul.

Others followed. In the movement's initial stages, these ascetics lived in small clusters within reasonable distance of a market for their produce and crafts and a place to buy food. Although they lived outside of and apart from towns and villages, they were economically associated with them. As the number of monks grew, more and more of them moved deeper into the desert. Some of the cells that had been used by other hermits were soon viewed as unsuitable because of their proximity to civilization. By 375 the monks had established communities in the deserts of the Nile valley. While most of them lived in isolated cells, they gathered together for worship, for buying and selling, and to seek instruction from one another.

Their model of the ascetic ideal was St. Anthony. Like him, the potential hermit had to be a man mature in faith, humble, detached from the world in body and in mind. Since the Desert Fathers believed (as did the Jewish Pietists) that God's will was hidden as well as revealed, they developed additional, and sometimes severe, rules and practices for themselves in order to test and refine their individual souls. The goal of the solitary's life was spiritual contemplation, the unimpeded focus on God and God's will. Physical solitude and bodily renunciation were the prerequisites for this task. Fasting and self-mortification were common. Only mechanical and undistracting work, such as weaving baskets and mats out of palm leaves or reeds, was permitted. But not all of the monks had the strength of St. Anthony. The harshness and loneliness of the desert broke the spirits of many of them, driving some to strange behavior and even madness. The call to self-denial could easily mutate into the exaltation of suffering. Asceticism could warp into an end in itself instead of a means to one. This growing need for careful vigilance and tighter organization led directly to the beginning of Christian monasticism and its various orders.

The teachings of these ancient ascetics were collected in a volume known as the *Verba Seniorum, The Sayings of the Fathers.* While the various biographies that were later written on the lives of the Desert Fathers tend to be very dramatic, full of superhuman legends and accounts of miracles, the *Verba* are simple and plain, reports that were transmitted from mouth to mouth in the Coptic tradition until they were eventually written down. The stories and aphorisms were intended as straightforward answers to direct questions about the spiritual life—no complicated theological arguments or abstract principles can be found in the collection. Here is a sample of the sayings, grouped by some of the more common themes in the literature of the desert:

separation and detachment

Abbot Anthony said: Just as fish die if they remain on dry land so monks, remaining away from their cells, or dwelling with men of the world, lose their determination to persevere in solitary prayer. Therefore, just as the fish should go back to the sea, so we must return to our cells, lest remaining outside we forget to watch over ourselves interiorly.

Abbot Arsenius prayed to the Lord, saying: Lord, lead me to salvation. And a voice came to him, saying: Arsenius, fly from men and you shall be saved.

A certain brother went to Abbot Moses in Scete, and asked him for a good word. And the elder said to him: Go, sit in your cell, and your cell will teach you everything.

An elder said: The monk's cell is that furnace of Babylon in which the three children found the Son of God; but it is also the pillar of cloud, out of which God spoke to Moses.

struggles and temptations

Abbess Syncletica of holy memory said: There is labor and great struggle for the impious who are converted to God, but after that comes inexpressible joy. A man who wants to light a fire first is plagued by smoke, and the smoke drives him to tears, yet finally he gets the fire that he wants. So also it is written: Our God is a consuming fire. Hence we ought to light the divine fire in ourselves with labor and with tears.

Abbot Pastor said that Abbot John the Dwarf had prayed to the Lord and the Lord had taken away all his passions, so that he became impassible. And in this condition he went to one of the elders and said: You see before you a man who is completely at rest and has no more temptations. The elder said: Go and pray to the Lord to command some struggle to be stirred up in you, for the soul is matured only in battles. And when the temptations started up again he did not pray that the struggle be taken away from him, but only said: Lord, give me strength to get through the fight.

Abbot Pastor said: Just as bees are driven out by smoke, and their honey is taken away from them, so a life of ease drives out the fear of the Lord from man's soul and takes away all his good works.

The fathers used to say: If some temptation arises in the place where you dwell in the desert, do not leave that place in time of temptation. For if you leave it then, no matter where you go, you will find the same temptation waiting for you.

fasting and self-denial

Abbot John the Dwarf said: If a king wants to take a city whose citizens are hostile, he first captures the food and water of the inhabitants of the city, and when they are starving subdues them. So it is with gluttony. If a man is earnest in fasting and hunger, the enemies which trouble his soul will grow weak.

Abbot Poemen said: The only way to humble the soul is by eating less bread.

Abbot Hyperichius said: When the monk's body is dried up with fasting, it lifts his soul from the depths. Fasting dries up the channels down which worldly pleasures flow.

Abbot Agatho said: What need have I, in my cell, of the bread of men?

An old man made a resolution not to drink for forty days. And if ever he thirsted he washed a vessel and filled it with water and hung it in front of his eyes. And when the brothers asked him why he was doing this, he replied: So that if I do not taste what I long for and can see, my devotion will be greater and I shall be granted a greater reward by the Lord.

silence and humility

Abbot Anthony said: The man who abides in solitude and is silent is delivered from fighting three battles—those of hearing, speech, and sight. Then he will have but one battle to fight—the battle of the heart.

Abbot Pastor said: Any trial whatever that comes to you can be conquered by silence.

They said of Abbot Agatho that for three years he kept a pebble in his mouth, to teach himself silence.

A brother asked one of the elders: How does fear of the Lord get into a man? And the elder said: If a man have humility and poverty, and judge not another, that is how fear of the Lord gets into him.

One of the elders said: If you see a young monk by his own will climbing up into heaven, take him by the foot and throw him to the ground, because what he is doing is not good for him.

Abbot Pastor said: A man must breathe humility and the fear of God just as ceaselessly as he inhales and exhales the air.

These sayings are not just moral and spiritual teachings that were easy to memorize and pass down as part of the lore of the ascetic tradition. They were also believed to contain a prophetic quality. A hermit did not invent a saying, he *received* it. In this sense, the *Verba* have been treated by monks over the centuries as a series of miniature revelations, gifts from God that were disclosed to men who lived and died amid solitude and sand, at the edge of the world.

Like St. Anthony, the spiritual paradigm for the Desert Fathers, St. Catherine of Genoa (1447–1510) did not start out as an ascetic. Caterina Adorna was born into a wealthy, aristocratic family. She was married and worked for most of her life at a large hospital in Genoa. But Caterina also had a secret life, a life that became more visible—and more extreme—as she grew older. In between her duties at the hospital, she could often be found facedown on the floor in a small room, "like one dead," in a state of mystical rapture. Caterina was many things at once: a caretaker and a contemplative, a wife and a mystic.

Caterina's spiritual drives surfaced early on in her life. When she was just eight years old, Caterina began to do formal penance. She slept on a mat of straw, using a block of wood for a headrest. At twelve (like Mechthild of Magdeburg), Caterina had a powerful religious experience and tried the following year to enter a local Augustinian convent. She was turned away on the grounds that she was too young. Then things slid further downhill for her. A year after Caterina was denied admission to the convent, her father died. Now in the custody of her eldest brother, she was contracted in marriage at the age of fifteen to a member of another wealthy and powerful Genoese family, the Adornos. The young Caterina did not try to escape from her unwanted marital situation, as had other women mystics in the past (such as Catherine of Siena, who cut off all her hair, or Christina of Markyate, who hid herself for several years in a hermit's cell). She was caught between two worlds, the world of religious rapture she had glimpsed that day when she was twelve, and the world of marriage, work, and ordinary life.

The couple was poorly matched. Caterina's husband, Giuliano, was a gambler, partier, and adulterer; he fathered at least one illegitimate child. After ten years of marriage to Giuliano, Caterina became physically ill around Christmas of 1472 and was confined to her bed until the spring. Her sister, Limbania, was a nun at the convent Caterina had tried to enter more than a decade earlier. Pained by her sister's condition, Limbania brought her to meet her own confessor. As Caterina knelt before the priest, a torrent of emotion flowed out of her. She felt a flash of God's love, a "wound to the heart" that was, simultaneously, an awareness of her own misery, weaknesses, and shortcomings as well as an awareness of God's ultimate benevolence and compassion. When the priest was called away, Caterina declared, "No more world! No more sins!"

Caterina believed that she had chosen despair over joy, resignation over religious life. She returned home filled with self-loathing, locking herself in a secluded room. In her book, *Purgation and Purgatory,* St. Catherine describes what it was like as her soul was gradually refined "in the fire of God's love." In the weeks after this experience, she writes that she looked more like a "frightened animal" than a human being yet acknowledges that the terror and pain of her self-awareness was necessary for her inner advancement. Caterina resolved to commit herself to spiritual pursuits, to a life with God. For the next four years she severed herself from the world of mundane chores and activities and subjected herself to a regimen of intense severity. She prayed six hours a day, wore an uncomfortable hair shirt, abstained from meat and fruit, ate other foods only if they had first been sprinkled with bitter herbs, fasted, and withdrew in silence from those around her. Caterina tried, through often painful external practices, to wash away the imperfections inside her, to bring her soul into closer alignment with God by removing the flaws that prevented their union.

After this period of spiritual refinement, Caterina returned to a less extreme way of life, beginning her association with the Ladies of Mercy hospital and working in Genoa's slums. But her ascetic drives never left her. On some days the only food she would eat was the consecrated wafer she received at the morning mass. One story even has her placing pieces of filth into her mouth from the houses of the poor she visited in order to condition herself against feeling disgust in the presence of those she tried to serve. In addition to her work with the sick and impoverished, Caterina also remained married (though by this point her husband had undergone a conversion himself, and their marriage appears to have been a chaste one from then on). Unwilling to abandon her professional and personal responsibilities despite her commitment to God, she decided to live with this tension, to withdraw from "normal" life while still participating in a world that sometimes challenged her devotion. Caterina lived and worked with Giuliano for another twenty years, striving to the end to fuse the active and the contemplative life into a singular expression of spiritual devotion.

Like St. Catherine, many spiritually inclined people have found that the imposition of mortifications and strictures on their external life, over which they can exert some control, helps to balance and contain the struggles that often occur internally as they reach for the spiritual ideal. These practices do not have to be a permanent feature of our lives; there is a rich tradition, from the era of the Nazir to our own day, of "temporary" asceticism, of taking a pause from ordinary life and devoting a period of time to inner development through outer discipline. That was why I went on my vision quest and why countless others have taken part in (sometimes unusual and harrowing) ascetic rituals that seem to outsiders more like acts of punishment than tools for interior transformation.

Judaism and Christianity approach asceticism in different ways. While certain ascetic practices and movements are clearly part of the Jewish spiritual tradition, moderation still seems to win out as the guiding religious principle. The idea of lifelong celibacy, for instance, is rejected in favor of either temporary abstinence or what might be called "ordered" sexuality, whereby sex is permitted, but only in specific situations and for specific reasons (such as procreation). Judaism recognizes the ascetic impulse but accepts it as religiously valid only within the context of a communal, institutionalized discipline. This can create a tension between the desires of those who strive for spiritual perfection and their ability to achieve that end. Yet it helps to rein in an asceticism beyond the pale of custom and law that can threaten separatism within a religion that is so communally oriented. In classical Christianity, however, and even in today's Catholicism, separatism and self-denial are built into the very fabric of religious life. While the various orders (Jesuits, Benedictines, Paulists) and offices (bishops, priests, nuns) have different missions and responsibilities, all of them share certain ascetic commitments (such as the vow of celibacy or poverty). Whereas in Judaism some of these practices exist as temporary disciplines, in Christianity they are often permanent modes of living meant to mirror the life of Jesus.

Asceticism is a powerful spiritual tool, but it must be kept in check. There can be negative aspects to asceticism. Depending on our personalities and proclivities, its rites, rituals, and practices can easily be used in the service of self-hatred and self-abuse. Social isolation can lead to misanthropy. Extreme, excessive preoccupation with God can mutate into disregard for the world. Religious history is, unfortunately, filled with examples of the perverse and pathological ways that asceticism can damage the human soul. Still, when kept in the proper perspective and utilized appropriately, ascetic acts—despite, or perhaps because of, their inherent discomfort—can serve as effective vehicles for spiritual insight and growth. Our challenge is to have minds that are open enough to appreciate the many, varied, and sometimes bizarre paths to God that we have inherited over the ages and that we continually create.

5 / on the silk road

Were this world an endless plain, and by sailing eastward we could for ever reach new distances, and discover sights more sweet and strange than any Cyclades or Islands of King Solomon, then there were promise in the voyage. But in pursuit of those far mysteries we dream of, or in tormented chase of that demon phantom that, some time or other, swims before all human hearts; while chasing such over this round globe, they either lead us on in barren mazes or midway leave us whelmed.

HERMAN MELVILLE, *Moby-Dick*

I've always been drawn to the world's edges. Even as a child, before I was ready to explore the Himalayas or the Arctic, I took journeys to distant lands through the pictures and maps in storybooks and atlases. When I grew older and began to experience the birth pangs of adult life, I became attracted to Nietzsche's famous dictum "That which does not kill you can only make you stronger." I think that in my mind the call of the wild and the concept of a trial are intertwined. This crystallized for me the summer before my final year of rabbinical school, when I felt an intense need to find a frontier, to test myself at the edge. In one more year I'd be ordained a rabbi. Was my soul ready? I'd spent twenty-seven years of my life devoted to the gratification of my own desires and impulses. Was I really committed to giving that up, to becoming a servant of my people and my God? How far was I willing to go in order to know the truth?

Over the years I'd heard many exotic tales from Jesuit friends about their missionary work in places like India and Africa, and since the Jewish seminaries didn't offer such valuable opportunities to their students, I figured I'd thumb my nose at their myopia and create my own mission to a region as remote as possible: Central Asia. For weeks I raised money from local synagogues. A human rights organization, the Union of Councils for Soviet Jewry, helped me map out an itinerary and establish contacts overseas. Documents were processed. Immunizations were received. Box after box began arriving at my apartment in Brooklyn, each one a grab bag of humanitarian aid: bandages, disinfectants, pens, notepads, prayer books, Bibles. My task was to repack them all into two or three manageable pieces I could carry with me on my travels. I was so weighed down the night I left that I did little more than shuffle through JFK Airport. I felt like a packhorse. Or a Jewish Santa Claus.

I wrote my first journal entry while I was still in the air: *I'm restless. I'm alone. I don't even know where my next bed will be. The Wandering Jew.* Though facing a challenge was the primary motivation for this mission, I was nervous. I spoke no Russian (my first stop was Moscow), nor any other language of the countries I'd be visiting. For communication, transportation, and accommodation, my life was in the hands of other people, faceless Jews I'd never met. More than ever before I would be dependent on the kindness of strangers, and I hated it. Up until this trip I'd viewed myself as a "true" American, a rugged individualist who didn't need anybody for anything. I was young and strong, I told myself. The world be damned. Now those words sounded idiotic.

On the ground in Moscow, I immediately spotted my hosts, Maya and Valentin, who were an older couple. It was 1993. Though opportunities were beginning to open up for the younger generation of Moscovites, it was too late for these two. They had food to eat, but that was all. Their professional lives—she was a physician and he was an engineer—were over. They'd been social activists, and the forces of repression and anti-Semitism had prevented their once promising careers from blooming. Back at their apartment they stuffed me with radishes, fruitcake, and vodka. I heard their stories. I told some stories of my own. We raised our glasses and toasted each other. I hadn't slept in a day and a half. Valentin wanted to keep drinking, but Maya prepared the couch for me. She tucked me in as if I were their son.

None of the countries I was to visit had even existed until a year earlier, having been Muslim republics in a now defunct Soviet Union. From New York, the only visa I was able to procure was for Russia, so the next day Valentin and I took the Metro to the Uzbek embassy to obtain the proper paperwork. I was greeted with suspicion and told that it would take weeks for a visa. Getting the right documents for the other countries, Kazakstan and Kyrgyzstan, turned out to be a problem as well, and to make matters worse, none of the officials seemed to know how I could do it or expressed any interest in helping me. I was faced with a dilemma: Either scrub the entire project and return to the United States or take my chances and head into Central Asia illegally. It was a tough call. But I remembered my mission, my *other* mission. Why would I run away from hardship now? Wasn't that the whole point of this thing? After another two days in Moscow—and close to half a day in the local Aeroflot office, trying to straighten out my tickets—I said good-bye to my hosts.

My flight left at midnight. I arrived at the airport several hours early and was directed to the "accumulation" area, a special place for foreigners traveling within the FSU (former Soviet Union). The room was so dark that it made everyone in it—many of whom looked suspicious already—seem shadowy. An air of dread mingled with the smell of urine. I noticed a man in a suit on the other side of the room who didn't quite seem to fit in. As we lined up for our flight, I looked at him more closely and saw that he was wearing a Peace Corps button on his lapel. We started talking and wound up being seated next to one another, either by chance or design (everything during my trip began to feel as if it were the result of some grand, invisible plan).

The American turned out to be the director of the Peace Corps in Kyrgyzstan. A middle-aged Connecticut Republican with five kids in college, he was clearly very wealthy—he'd run a bank and owned a marina until he decided to give it all up for this. He got the job, it appeared, through his connections in Washington. We spoke for hours, and he gave me all sorts of useful information about Central Asia as well as some tips on how to deal with my visa problems. (It crossed my mind that his story was a sham and that he was really a CIA operative.) By three or four we became more self-revelatory, as strangers traveling alone often do when they meet in the middle of nowhere and will never see each other again. He talked about how much he missed his sons, and I explained my difficulties in establishing emotional connections with my father. He told me not to wait and then told me of his own absent, alcoholic father. He'd never fall prey to that darkness, he said.

As faint rays of light began to penetrate our cabin, somber stewardesses brought us our breakfast: bread, salami, and horrific pieces of what I think was chicken. Even though I was a vegetarian, I ate the meal. (I knew I'd have little choice about my food for the rest of the summer.) We arrived in Kazakstan at dawn, just as the sun was beginning to disclose the Kyzyl-Kum desert below and the Tien Shan mountains to the east. The Silk Road. Land of mystery and danger. Though my ostensible purpose was to visit the Jewish communities of Central Asia, teaching, performing rabbinic functions, gathering information on those trying to emigrate, and distributing cash, religious articles, and medicine to my contacts, I also had my hidden purpose, my test. I was exactly where I was supposed to be. When the plane landed I lumbered down to the tarmac, a duffel bag crammed with medicine slung over my right shoulder and a box of books and school supplies cradled under my left. I felt as though I were wearing a scarlet *A* on my chest—"American"—and an *I* on my back—"Illegal."

No one checked my papers at the Almaty airport. There were no border controls whatsoever. My Peace Corps friend was right—it was truly the Wild East. With the city's wide array of nationalities—Kazaks, Russians, Ukrainians, Tatars, Turkmens, Tajiks—it was easy to become anonymous, as long as nobody asked me any questions. The American wished me luck and disappeared into the crowd. Once inside the terminal, I looked for my contacts, Itta and Natasha. I couldn't find them and was hit with a wave of panic. I didn't even know how to make a phone call, let alone get by on my own. Then I heard someone call out in Hebrew: *Shalom! Shalom!* Just ahead of me, waving feverishly to get my attention, were two dark, petite, smiling women and an enormous man with a cap that made him look like some monstrous version of Robin Hood. They were holding up a sheet of paper with RABI NILE GOLDSTEIN scrawled awkwardly across it.

The Kazaks, proud, nomadic people supposedly descended from the Mongol hordes that swept across Central Asia, were again in control of their own destinies. Kazak nationalism, growing Islamic fundamentalism, and constant pressure from Christian missionaries all contributed to a sense of unease among the Jewish population. A civil war was taking place just to the south in Tajikistan. Economic conditions, in Almaty (the capital of Kazakstan) as in the rest of the FSU, were terrible. Everyone's chief concern was food. Yet the Jews, originally shipped to the region by Stalin, also worried about the survival of their children. Even though the Soviet system had collapsed, religious freedom didn't feel all that free to the Jews. While I was there we held services in a photography studio. As I began the evening prayers, someone would always close the shutters on the windows and lock the front door. I never felt in immediate danger, but I never felt at ease.

I stayed at the home of the enormous man, Simon, a former major in the Soviet air force. To my surprise, he and his wife, Diana, offered me their bed, but I declined and slept on their back porch. Itta and her daughter, Natasha, were my guides and translators, and they were the ones who arranged all of my work within the Jewish community. Simon was a character. Though he was as compassionate and generous as anyone I'd ever known, he had a habit of issuing orders to everyone around him, including me, as if we were his subordinates. Simon had been a helicopter pilot but before that had been a POW during World War II. I tried to get him to talk about his experiences, but he kept changing the subject.

As Natasha tried to resolve my visa problems, I started serving as Almaty's rabbi-in-residence. In addition to leading services and giving lectures, I spent a lot of time with a young man, Klim, who had recently lost his mother. Klim had no relationship with his father and no friends to speak of—he felt alone in the world. With Itta's help, I tried to console him. Mostly I just listened, to his words of grief and pain, to his doubts about God and even about the value of life itself. We visited his mother's grave, and I helped him to say the Kaddish for her. I suggested at one point that he put on a pair of tefillin that I'd brought with me from Brooklyn. Klim placed one box on his arm and the other one over his head. He began to cry. Soon I did, too. Then the two of us prayed together. And I wondered which one of us was really helping the other.

I went with Itta one day to a run-down apartment building near the edge of the city. She wanted me to pay a visit to a woman who was poor, sick, and unable to get around on her own. The staircase was musty and dark, and her apartment was on the top floor.

I kissed the mezuzah on her doorpost as I entered—it had been nailed on incorrectly, but it seemed absurd to me to even think of pointing that out. Despite the gloom around her, the woman's face glowed with a softness that seemed to suffuse the whole room. After Itta explained why I was there and gave her some of the medicine I'd brought with me, the woman, whose diabetes had taken her legs and consigned her to a wheelchair, smiled and embraced me. Though she was going blind, her eyes were filled with faith. Her wish was to die in Israel, but she couldn't make it there alone. She was about the same age as my mother. I realized that in America, where there was proper health care, none of these problems was likely to have developed. I also realized that it was an accident of history that had brought my mother's parents to Milwaukee (from their childhood homes in the Ukraine) and had led—through her own parents' choices—to this woman's misery and misfortune in Kazakstan. She could have been my mother. I felt grateful. I also felt enraged at the injustice.

There was a biologist in the community who was about to move to Israel with his three sons. Their Jewish identities were strong, but their lineage was somewhat ambiguous; he wanted to have all of them undergo circumcision before their arrival in the Holy Land so there would be no problems with immigration and so they would be, as he phrased it, "real Jews." Since none of the four men were babies, the bris ceremony had to be adapted to the needs of the situation. With the help of Itta and Natasha, we gathered a minyan, a quorum of ten members of the Jewish community, and huddled together in surgical gowns and face masks in the back of an operating room. I would recite the blessings while a (Muslim) Kazak anesthesiologist would put each of them under; a Jewish surgeon performed the actual operation. One by one we wheeled them in, and he removed their foreskins. After I said the appropriate blessings, I leaned over to place a drop of wine onto their lips, the fringes of my prayer shawl brushing against the steel table. I visited them in their apartment a couple of days later. All four of them had towels wrapped around their waists. They thanked me and told me that even though they couldn't remember it, the bris was the most meaningful thing that had ever happened to them.

Toward the end of my stay, Simon and I were sitting one evening at his kitchen table, drinking tea. He was a hard man to fathom, but we'd both become more comfortable with each other over the past weeks. I decided to ask him about his wartime experiences one last time. This time he answered. He told me how, at the age of eight, he was dragged with his mother by the Nazis to a camp somewhere in the Ukraine. Many of the other Jews from their town who were rounded up with them died during the march. Most of the rest died in the camp from typhus, starvation, or shooting by the Nazis. Out of a town with 5,000 Jews, fewer than 150 survived the war. Simon was one of them. So was his mother, who died in the Ukraine a decade later. Simon described his solemn and solitary visits back to her grave. When I asked about his father, he was silent. I asked him again. Then he told me how the Nazis had herded many of the men from the town into a small church and gunned them down. His father was among them. As he was telling me about his father, Simon's voice suddenly cracked. He could no longer speak. Dwarfing me as he rose from the table, he walked out onto the back porch. After a few minutes I touched his arm and said, "I'm sorry." I didn't feel like a rabbi. I felt like a jackass.

Soon it was time for me to move on to Bishkek, the capital of Kyrgyzstan. Days before, I'd been officially *dis*invited by the leader of Bishkek's Jewish community, partly because I was a Reform rabbi (and a member of a movement that most Jews in Central Asia had never heard of or, owing to negative propaganda by certain Orthodox groups, considered anathema) and partly because he'd heard I was traveling without any papers. At my insistence, my contacts and I nevertheless established links with other Jews in the community who promised they'd receive me and set up a few "underground" lectures. After trying all morning to dissuade me from making the journey to Bishkek, wondering why in the world I'd want to travel illegally to a place I wasn't wanted, Itta, Natasha, and Simon put me onto a bus at the central station.

When we reached the border between Kazakstan and Kyrgyzstan, soldiers entered the bus. I'd been told that they were looking mostly for drugs and contraband—the mountainous region is a hotbed of narcotics activity—but I worried that they'd ask me for my papers. With nothing but a Russian visa, and unable to speak the language, I wondered how I'd be able to defend myself. This was by far the worst aspect of my visit to Central Asia: the border crossings. At best they made me feel uneasy; at worst they filled me with a fear that I'd be discovered and arrested. After asking some of the others for their documents, and checking under our seats for anything that seemed suspicious, the soldiers waved us through. I took a deep breath. Kyrgyz horsemen watched us from a nearby hillside, their colorful saddlebags standing out against the stark brown slopes.

I was sitting next to a band of muscular and tattooed Russian men. As we got closer to Bishkek, they offered me some of the homemade vodka that they'd been guzzling throughout the trip (they'd also been grilling sticks of kebab between us in the aisle). I refused, but they kept pressing it on me. Soon I saw that I had no choice. Not wanting to offend them, and sensing that my black belt in karate probably wouldn't do me much good against them if the scene turned ugly, I accepted their gift. The vodka tasted like rubbing alcohol, but after a few more passes of the bottle it didn't really matter anymore. I arrived in Bishkek with a buzz, wandering through its central station for more than an hour before my contact was able to find me.

Nayira, the fiery daughter of an Armenian father and a Jewish mother, brought me back to her apartment and introduced me to her husband, Igor, a psychophysiologist. The two of us hit it off immediately, discussing (mostly through grunts and nods) Hegel, Freud, and Martin Buber. Igor's mother was an English teacher. She joined us for dinner, and through her help I learned that the Jews of Kyrgyzstan were confronting most of the same problems that the Jews in Kazakstan faced. There was a famine in the nation's southern region. Many of Bishkek's younger Jews had managed to emigrate to Israel with the help of their parents. A few days later, on his birthday, Nayira and Igor got a call from their oldest son in Tel Aviv. They spoke for three minutes. They hadn't seen him in two years.

I spent most of my time in Bishkek meeting with members of the Jewish community. None of their leaders—who I was told were corrupt—would talk to me. Nayira arranged for me to go on a drive into the mountains with a friend of hers, an unemployed Tatar dentist. The man was also a veteran of the war in Afghanistan, a former special forces commando who saw a year of combat there. We drove into the foothills of the Ala Tau Range, across tundra, past grazing sheep, beneath snow-capped peaks. Occasionally we'd pass a yurt. My escort tried to tell me (with some English he remembered from high school) about the nomadic life of the Kyrgyz. On the way back into town, he pulled off at a cemetery. Leading me to its military section, he showed me the grave of a friend who had stepped on a mine in Afghanistan, just yards ahead of him. His eyes grew glassy. I left him alone and returned to the car.

The last nation I planned to go to was Uzbekistan. During my stay in Bishkek I met with some of the exiled leaders of that country's political opposition as well as with other human rights activists familiar with the situation there. Based on their experiences and the background information I'd studied prior to my trip, it was clear that Uzbekistan wasn't a particularly pleasant place to visit. Still, I had two garbage bags labeled TASHKENT and SAMARKAND stuffed with medicine and supplies, and I wasn't going to leave Central Asia without at least trying to get them into the hands of my contacts.

The American embassy in Bishkek had just opened its doors. Literally. I walked right in, past half-opened boxes of computers and fax machines. Aside from me, the handful of people in the office were probably the only other native English speakers in the entire nation. I identified myself and wound up schmoozing with a diplomat about Park Slope, the neighborhood where I lived and the place his son was about to move to. After a few minutes I met with the ambassador, who happened to be Jewish. I explained the purpose of my trip, the problems I'd had with documentation, and my determination to enter Uzbekistan, despite my concerns about safety.

I asked for his advice. He warned me not to go there without an official visa, that if I were caught, I could be in real trouble. Yet waiting in Bishkek for a proper visa would have taken weeks, and I had to return to Moscow relatively soon to catch my flight home. He told me that if I flew to Uzbekistan, I would almost certainly be stopped and questioned at the airport, and that the trains were too dangerous because of holdups. Taking a bus, as I'd done to enter Kyrgyzstan, was the least conspicuous and least risky alternative. I thanked the ambassador, and he wished me luck. "You're on your own," he said.

Nayira and Igor bought me a ticket for the evening bus from Bishkek to Tashkent. It was pouring rain outside, and none of us had umbrellas. They waited with me for two hours under a rusted steel shelter for the bus to arrive. Then they told the Kyrgyz man who was sitting next to me—I inferred from their gestures—to keep an eye on me, that I was a foreigner who didn't speak the language. That eased some of my fear. It was a ten-hour trip to the Uzbek capital, much of it through the desert. The bus would cross two different borders (from Kyrgyzstan back to Kazakstan and from Kazakstan to

Uzbekistan) before I'd reach my destination. I accepted a bag of fruit and a jug of water from my hosts, then waved good-bye.

Every hour or so a group of border guards with assault rifles boarded the bus. The Kyrgyz man whispered in my ear, "Not to talking. This cops." I shut my eyes and pretended to be asleep as they walked down the aisle, but inside I was awake and terrified. The soldiers checked the papers of a few men, even made a couple of them get off the bus for questioning. I started to sweat. No scenario I could construct made any sense—I was screwed no matter what I did. The soldiers never did question me, though. In between checkpoints I tried to rest, but I couldn't. We pulled off the highway intermittently to use the toilets—rows of holes in dark, concrete huts. When it was time to depart again, my Kyrgyz friend always made sure I wasn't left behind. We exchanged few words during the journey. Mostly gestures and nervous smiles.

It was close to sunrise when we reached the outskirts of Uzbekistan. As we slowed down for the final checkpoint, my heart was pounding. The guards climbed onto the bus, their AK-47s clanging against the steps. They asked the driver some questions and examined his documents. One of them looked back and caught me staring at him. It scared the hell out of me. For an instant, time froze. I was face-to-face with the Other, a foreign figure in total control of my fate. That soldier was my whole world, my momentary god. Yet when he turned away, I realized that as important as he was to me, I meant nothing to him. I've never felt so relieved by my own insignificance. The guards climbed off the bus and waved us through, and we crossed the border into the Uzbek nation.

Soon we were in downtown Tashkent. As we all gathered our baggage from the bus, the Kyrgyz man approached me and smiled. We shook hands. I wanted to thank him, but I didn't know how. Before I could open my mouth, he turned and disappeared into the crowd outside. I was alone, exhausted, and anxious—I felt as if I'd just entered the belly of some great beast. I wrote in my journal: *The fear I feel is matched only by my excitement.* (I wondered whether this mission wasn't rooted more in the selfish craving for an adrenaline rush than in altruism.) Someone tapped me on the shoulder from behind. It was Misha, my new contact. He was the one who'd take me the rest of the way to Samarkand. Once inside his car, we drove silently through the blistering desert, twice being pulled over by local policemen (whom Misha bribed into letting us pass). There were clusters of soldiers up and down the highway. Hours later, as the sun began to set, we stopped by the side of the road to buy some fresh *kvass* from the back of a truck. The oasis town of Samarkand was just a few miles ahead.

Samarkand is one of the oldest cities in the world, dating back thousands of years. It was used as a main stop along the Silk Road as the ancient Greeks transported the treasures of the Far East back to their empire. The Jews of Samarkand, the Bukharans, trace their ancestry to the Babylonian exile. I felt as though I were going back in time as we began the climb into town. It was a Friday afternoon, and the Sabbath was near. We bought warm loaves of bread with dill and a jar of honey from a roadside vendor. Making a final ascent up a hill, in the shadow of minarets, we entered Samarkand. Misha wanted me to get a glimpse of the old city, the *mahallah,* before we went to his home for our Sabbath meal. We drove through the narrow streets and alleyways of the Jewish quarter, past a synagogue and bathhouse. It was something out of the Middle Ages.

I spotted a man dressed in black and wearing a hasidic fedora, looking totally out of place in this Islamic town. Misha picked him up. Since he was an Israeli and spoke Hebrew, I was able to converse with him. He was a Jewish missionary, like me; he was in Samarkand for the summer to teach Hebrew but lived and studied with the

Lubavitch movement back in Crown Heights, Brooklyn. *Brooklyn!* Rather than welcoming his company, I resented him. He was an intruder in my fantasy, and I couldn't wait for him to get out of the car. When we reached Misha's home (the first actual house I'd seen in the FSU), I showered for the first time in five days. Most of the men in Samarkand—Jewish and Muslim—wore head coverings, so I put on mine and left it there during my stay. We had dinner in their courtyard. While Misha's wife and daughters toiled in the kitchen, his father asked me to say the blessing over the wine. Everything, from the grape leaves to the vodka to the lamb, was homemade and kosher. As hard as it was to be Jewish in the other areas I'd visited, in Samarkand it seemed easy. It was a Jewish Shangri-la, an oasis of Jewish identity in one of the world's most remote and isolated places.

The next morning I went to pray at one of the two local synagogues. Before the October Revolution there had been dozens of them, but now only the traces of the once powerful Bukharan community remained. Most of the worshippers were old men. They couldn't believe I was (almost) a rabbi. Where was my beard? After services I walked through the *mahallah*. Though the Jewish community in Samarkand was an intense one, it was also a community in its death throes. Most of the Jewish homes had been sold (usually at a great loss) to Muslims. Every night there were farewell parties for families who were leaving. Living under an oppressive government, with Islamic fundamentalism permeating the borders from nearby Iran and Afghanistan, and with the bloody civil war raging in neighboring Tajikistan, every Jew I met wanted to leave Uzbekistan. Their fear was almost palpable. After centuries of a robust cultural and economic life in Samarkand, the Bukharan community was coming to an end.

Toward the end of my stay I made a visit to the Jewish cemetery, which sat beneath the city's bazaars and blue-domed mosques. Groups of Jews, traveling in bands from grave to grave, paid their last respects to dead relatives. These people, I was told, would probably never set foot here again, never visit the graves of their parents or children. They brought along videocameras and filmed the event in an attempt to preserve this moment. I was watching yet another great Jewish migration and the destruction of one more great Jewish culture. There was something mythic about it. Here were my brothers and sisters, the wandering Jews, packing up and moving on. For me, there was a strange beauty in this tragedy, and I grasped then and there the root of my own wanderlust. Jews can't help but journey. It's in our bones.

Despite the sadness and fear of many of the Jews around me, I treated Samarkand like a playground, a fantasyland of faith and history. I stopped thinking, at least temporarily, about my legal status and let the city's spiritual exotica envelop me. In addition to the Jewish sites, Misha showed me the mausoleums of Shahi Zinda, tombs and mosques of glazed blue tiles built between the thirteenth and fifteenth centuries. I saw the Registan, a compound of three ancient *madrasas,* or koranic schools, that once served as the intellectual center of the Islamic world. I also visited the Gur Emir, the final resting place of the warlord Tamerlane, whose vast empire started in Samarkand and stretched across the whole of Central Asia. All that was left now was a jade tombstone. In the afternoons we'd eat cherries, sip tea, and swat flies in the courtyards of Misha's friends and relatives; in the evenings we'd feast on lamb and vodka. I'd given Misha the medicine and books when I arrived in town, and the Bukharans seemed to have little need for my insights on Judaism. I was having a lot of fun, but I was starting to feel irrelevant.

Perhaps picking up on this, Misha arranged for me to give a lecture on Jewish history at the public library. Most of the Jews who showed up for my talk were of European descent—the Bukharans rarely associated with these twentieth-century "newcomers." Knowing no Russian, and unable to speak in the Judeo-Tajik language of

Samarkand's Jews, I gave the lecture in Hebrew (my translator didn't know English). I noticed a beautiful blond woman sitting toward the back of the room but pretended to ignore her as I spoke. At the end of my lecture she approached me. She told me—through my interpreter—of her need to find a more accessible and egalitarian religious alternative to the Orthodox monopoly in Samarkand and thanked me for describing some of the differences in the various Jewish movements that emerged after the Enlightenment.

Later that afternoon Misha knocked on the door to my room and told me that someone wanted to speak with me. He said something about my passport, but since I carried it with me wherever I went, I didn't pay much attention. When I walked through the courtyard and up to the entrance of his home, I saw a man in a uniform standing on the sidewalk. He demanded my passport. Misha conveyed to me that this man, who spoke no English, of course, was an officer from Ovir, the FSU's visa control agency. I was shocked. How could they have known? Someone had to have informed on me. Probably a Jew—from the synagogue or maybe from the library. Someone had betrayed me. The bastard. The officer fingered through the pages of my passport and told me that I was in Uzbekistan illegally. He confiscated my passport and ordered me to report to Ovir's headquarters the next morning. I felt violated and exposed. I also felt powerless. Misha brought me back inside and told me not to worry.

I could barely speak. Here I was, a young rabbinical student traveling alone near a war zone, trying to do nothing more (as far as they knew) than help other Jews, and some son of a bitch turns me in to the police. Misha managed to calm me down. He told me that this kind of thing happened all the time, that it was a key part of the Soviet system, that if I tried to figure out how exactly they had come to know what they knew, I'd drive myself crazy. People will do anything for a few rubles or to curry favor with the authorities, he said. We'd just tell them I was an American guest and that I had made a simple mistake. But I had visions of serving time. I tried to plan how I'd make up my coursework at the end of eight or ten months in an Uzbek prison. Misha told me to relax. Then he told me how, while I was in my room, he'd arranged for me to spend the evening with the woman I'd seen at the library.

Her name was Irina. She was the granddaughter of one of Samarkand's most famous Bukharan masters of the *shash maqam,* the classical music style of the region. She lived in the heart of the *mahallah,* near the bathhouse, with her mother and daughter (from a previous relationship). Misha had told them, under some pretense, that I needed a place to sleep for the night, so they had invited me over for dinner. I showed up at their home with a couple of bottles of cognac tucked under my arm. The family had a friend who spoke English, so he joined us at the table to translate our conversation. We spoke about Judaism, Israel, and America. They were very interested in talking about those things, but it felt like a sham. I knew why I was really there.

By midnight their friend had left, and Irina's mother, who'd said absolutely nothing during the meal, went to bed. The daughter was already asleep. Irina and I sat alone in her living room. She was almost ten years older than me, but she was the most beautiful and exotic woman I'd seen in all of Samarkand: half-Bukharan, half-Russian. We struggled to communicate. Somehow I managed to ask her to put on a tape of her grandfather's music. It was like nothing I'd ever heard before, rhythms and voices that could only have come from the desert. Irina took out a children's book. She was going to teach me Russian. As she taught me the Cyrillic alphabet, she'd intermittently place her hand on my thigh. *This thing is actually happening,* I thought. I wasn't sure what to do. Wasn't I there as a religious servant? If I crossed that line, wouldn't I be nothing more than a fraud?

Our awkward exchange turned next to the subject of sex. She asked me to explain the seduction process using English words. I wrote up a list of stages for her: *Touch. Caress. Kiss. Excite. Act.* (I also wrote after them *Cigarette. Sleep.*) Irina listed the similar terms in Russian and casually proceeded to demonstrate on my arm just what a "caress" was. I looked deep into her brown eyes. "You're in total control of this situation," I said, knowing perfectly well that she wouldn't understand me. It was all smoke and mirrors, and we both knew it. She didn't want to learn English, and I didn't want to learn Russian. Neither of us said anything for a long time. Then Irina broke the silence. "What you want?" she asked. I answered that I wanted her. "You very *dangerous* man," she said.

I woke up in a cold sweat—not because of what had happened between me and Irina, but because I had to get to the Ovir office in less than an hour. Her mother wouldn't let me leave before I'd had some tea. I thanked her for everything, and I told Irina that I'd get in touch with her after my meeting. But I was scared to death. I didn't know what was going to happen to me in that office. Misha picked me up in his car and drove with me to the Ovir headquarters. We concocted a story that would make my illegal status seem more innocent, yet the two of us were separated the moment we entered the building. I decided to think twice before telling any lies. There were three people waiting for me as I was led into an office: the Ovir officer, an interpreter, and a man with a pockmarked face who sat to the side of the desk. I sat on a chair in the middle of the room, directly in front of my interrogators.

In a very calm voice, the man off to the side asked me the questions, while the officer, a colonel, was reduced to the level of a clerk as he wrote down my answers. How did I get to Samarkand? What was the purpose of my visit? Who did I know? Who helped me? Why was

I there without a visa? I answered as best I could, claiming that it was all a simple misunderstanding, that I thought I needed a visa only for Russia in order to travel through Central Asia. The man reminded me that the Soviet Union no longer existed. "I'm a religious man," I said, pointing to my yarmulke. "I would never knowingly break the laws of a foreign country." I had the sensation that he was seeing right through me. I was terrified. If this was my test, I wanted it to end already.

It all seemed surreal. Had my desire to find the frontier brought me to the edge of disaster? Had I traveled halfway across the globe to confirm my calling or to escape from it? The pockmarked man said a few words in Russian to the colonel, who nodded his head and spoke, reading from what looked like a large legal book: "Rabbi Niles Goldstein, having violated law 1253 under criminal code 57b of the Republic of Uzbekistan, you must hereby . . ." My worst nightmare had come true. I'd been caught in the act, and I was heading to jail—just like before. All the unpleasant memories of the Tombs came back to me in a flash. ". . . pay a fine in the amount of seventy-five thousand rubles to the Uzbek government and then leave the country immediately." It was as if God had stepped in. I'd been spared. Misha was brought into the room, and they explained to him what had just happened. The fine (which Misha paid after withdrawing money from a bank until I could repay him later in the day) amounted to a six-month salary in the FSU, but to me it was about the price of a dinner for two in a Manhattan restaurant. In a final gesture of absurdity, I thanked the three officials and shook their hands.

Misha told me in the car that the pockmarked man was a KGB agent. He also told me that he'd been able to knock down the fine to forty thousand rubles and that he'd bribed the Ovir officer so that I could stick around a couple of more days. He handed me my passport. I was still a nervous wreck, barely able to fathom what had just transpired and afraid of every uniform I saw. Misha told me to relax, that it was all over now. I wanted to kiss him. That evening after dinner I contacted Irina and arranged to spend the night at her place again. I wanted to return to the mystical *mahallah,* to the shadows and alleyways and donkey carts that would take me away from everything on this side of its whitewashed walls.

Irina's family was asleep by the time I arrived. She asked how things had gone in the morning, and I said they had gone fine. The two of us went into her kitchen. Irina made tea and I drank vodka. She wore a thin bathrobe that revealed the full shape of her body and exposed her dark, smooth skin. I couldn't believe how beautiful she looked. She told me of the great "tragedy" of her life: her inability to find a home. She'd been married to a man ten years before, but the marriage had lasted only for a few months. His love for her drove him mad, she said. Several years later she met someone else, her daughter's father, but the two of them never married. All of the men in her life had acted like "little boys," and many others wanted her. None had been mature enough to keep her. Irina was now involved with a twenty-four-year-old Uzbek saxophone player who was crazy about her, but she didn't want to marry a Muslim. Yet because her mother was Russian, none of the Jewish men would marry her, either. She felt trapped by her birth and destined to be alone.

Smiling knowingly, she asked me about my life. I told her of my need for adventure, my struggles with responsibility, my hatred of limitations and fear of death. I told her that I wanted to be a rabbi, but that I was afraid becoming a rabbi would mean I could no longer be a man—at least the kind of man I wanted to be. How could I be a writer, an explorer, a lover—and simultaneously devote my soul to a people and a faith? How could I be a libertine and at the same time constrain myself with religious commandments? I couldn't do everything, but I wasn't going to give up without a fight. This was my tragedy: an inability to find peace.

Irina laughed. She *laughed* at me. "You very funny man," she said, unable to believe that I was really going to be a rabbi. My heart felt as if it had been ripped out of my ribs. I wanted to get up from the table and run away from her, from the *mahallah,* from myself. I was ashamed, desperate. Unable to say anything, I simply stared at her. And then something happened. Something terrifying. Through my haze of alcohol and angst, Irina no longer seemed human. Her face darkened. Her eyes grew severe. She began to change into some kind of beast or demon. I was convinced she'd been sent from hell to taunt me, test me. I was a failure, a lost soul. "You no know love," she said. Her words sank into me. How could she have known? *How?* Then, just as suddenly as she'd become a devil, Irina transformed into an angel, shimmering with light, sent by God to help me, to show me my shortfalls, and to hint at the key to my redemption. Still smiling, she took my hand and, turning off the light, led me out of the kitchen.

Within days I was back in Moscow and preparing for my return flight to New York. Everything about Samarkand started to feel like a dream. But something was revealed to me that night, something I couldn't shake off. I think it was my humanity. I'd come to Central Asia to test myself, to confront my spiritual mettle. Had I passed? I wasn't sure one way or the other. Was I ready to be a rabbi? I didn't know. What I did know was that no matter how far I journeyed, the same demons and the same angels that I'd seen on the Silk Road would journey with me. Irina was a mirror of my inner conflicts. I longed for her, but I knew that I could never see her again. The *mahallah* was too real to bear, almost too real to be real, and if I were to return to it, I would either kill its magic or lose my soul. The call of the wild had led me to a great desert thousands of miles from home. But the call of my faith was stronger.

I had other regions to explore.

I am not alone. For ages men and women have found their spiritual callings not in the familiar, comfortable centers of their religious institutions, but at the geographic peripheries. As I myself can attest, those who are drawn to this kind of religious expression often have complicated and sometimes contradictory motivations: a selfless desire to help those on the margins, a personal love of physical adventure, a passion to explore new frontiers. Nowhere in the Christian and Jewish traditions is this impulse more apparent than in the lives and work of missionaries and maggids. While some of these individuals were forced into their roles as wanderers by practical necessity or through orders from a superior, others embraced—and frequently sought out—such opportunities. In a sense, many of these figures were able to spiritualize, almost sanctify, their wanderlust—a drive that does not always fit easily into the framework of organized religion or the commitments of community that it tries to engender.

From as far back as the New Testament, Christianity has advocated that its adherents "go out all over the world and preach the gospel to all creation." Jesus himself was an itinerant, traversing the Holy Land in order to teach his spiritual message. So was Paul, who traveled throughout the ancient Near East to promote the new Christian religion. Later, the monastic tradition developed orders that specialized in such evangelizing, such as the Franciscans and Dominicans. And some modern orders, like the Maryknolls, continue this ministry to foreign lands into our own day. The goal of the missionary was to save souls, to preach the gospel of Jesus, to spread

Christianity "all over the world." Taking the scriptural order literally, missionaries wandered far and wide, often braving harsh conditions, to do their work. As a Jew, I have never been comfortable with the idea or the effects of aggressive Christian proselytizing, but I have always found the contexts and settings for missionary activity romantic and compelling. One of the more colorful examples is that of the Jesuits—the "black robes"—in North America.

By the seventeenth century Spain had already established both a political and a religious presence in the New World. But the intertwined relationship between the Crown and the church in their colonization efforts had led to terrible abuses. For almost two hundred years the Spaniards had conquered, converted, or killed indigenous peoples in the Americas. As a result of these abuses, American Indians were not excited by the prospect of new missionaries from France entering the picture. Yet by 1650 the Jesuit order, riding the tide of a religious renewal in Europe and especially in France, had grown to fifteen thousand members. Its priests were spread across the globe, preaching the gospel to the Brahmins in India and the native peoples in Africa. So when France began its own exploration and colonization of North America, or "New France," as the French called it, the Jesuit missionaries were not far behind.

The Christian spirituality of this period focused on rigorous discipline and self-denial. This helps to explain the ability (and desire) of the black robes to suffer incredible hardships and even death itself in the most remote and lonely outposts in North America. Even if it meant "saving" just a single soul, these zealous Jesuits followed the Indians up and down rivers on foot and in canoes, over frozen lakes and trails buried in snow. Such physical challenges must have been daunting—but, on another level that I know very well from my own experiences as a seminarian and a young rabbi, uniquely appealing—to these European, university-educated priests. From morning until evening the black robes would discuss Christianity with their hosts. At night they slept side by side with their potential converts in shelters filled with smoke and smelling of disease. The bitter winters nearly froze them to death. "Suffering and hardship," one missionary wrote, "are the privileges of these holy but arduous Missions." Sometimes after months or even years of trying to preach the gospel to the Indians, the missionaries had succeeded in baptizing only a handful of them.

Many of the French Jesuits started their journeys at one of several permanent missions in Quebec. From these outposts they would fan out along the St. Lawrence River deep into the Canadian interior. One of the first tribes that the Jesuits approached was the Hurons (in Ontario). At the peak of their missionary activity, the priests reported that they were serving twelve thousand Indians and had performed more than a thousand baptisms—a far heavier workload than the standard one of my Jesuit contemporaries. They built a mission town, Sainte Marie, which became the center of the mission and the headquarters for the Jesuits. Each black robe was responsible for his own circuit of Huron villages and maintained his own rustic mission there. But there were many problems. In addition to finding that their conversion efforts were not always welcomed by the Indians, the Jesuits sometimes found themselves caught in intertribal hostilities, particularly the long-standing one between the Hurons and the Iroquois. During skirmishes and raids between these two tribes, several priests were taken prisoner, tortured, and put to death by the Iroquois. The killings of three of them—Isaac Jogues, Jean de Brebeuf, and Gabriel Lalemant—have become the stuff of Catholic legend.

After 1670 French expansionism brought explorers as well as missionaries south into the Mississippi valley and the western Great Lakes. Jacques Marquette was perhaps the most famous of the Jesuit missionaries to enter the American heartland. In less than a decade he explored the Mississippi with La Salle and founded three important missions—Sault Sainte Marie and St. Ignace on Michigan's Upper Peninsula, and Kaskaskia in Illinois. He also paved the way for future Catholic missionaries. A century later Jesuit "circuit riders" served small congregations in remote areas of the budding American nation. In 1770, for instance, Maryland was a rural colony comprised mainly of people living on farms that were scattered far apart from each other. One circuit rider, Joseph Mosley, divided his time among eight different communities of Catholic families. Alone and on horseback (without the relative "luxury" of the decrepit buses and shaky Aeroflot flights that took me from community to community in Central Asia), the itinerant Mosley would celebrate mass, preach, visit the sick, comfort the infirm, and administer the sacraments. His work was not as hazardous as that of his black robe predecessors in Canada, but it was not easy. Riding all day "in excessive heats, the use of bad water, salt meats, bad accommodations, violent colds, poor open lodging, often out whole nights in the woods" made this kind of religious mission a constant challenge.

Missionary work was also a key part of American Protestantism. Its various missionary enterprises emerged almost immediately in the seventeenth-century colonies from New England to Virginia, with "foreign" missions directed toward the Indians and home missions that targeted increasingly dispersed European settlers and their descendants. These missionary activities intensified as America grew. In 1798 the Connecticut Missionary Society was formed "to christianize the Heathen in North America, and to support and promote Christian knowledge in the new settlements, within the United States." Other societies followed. By 1826 the American Home Missionary Society was established in New York to consolidate their efforts. Many of its missionaries were a major force in the development of the West, not only as Protestant evangelists, but as educators, civic leaders, and exponents of East Coast culture. (Today the movement seems to be eastward: I have met Mormons proselytizing in downtown Brooklyn and Pentecostalists preaching in Nepal and Kazakstan.) In addition to these home missions, which focused on domestic concerns, there were also foreign missions, which concentrated on religious work abroad. In 1810, for example, a group of Connecticut and Massachusetts ministers created the powerful and long-lived American Board of Commissioners for Foreign Missions.

The home missions of the Congregationalists led to the creation of new parishes across the country and the founding of new seminaries in Chicago (1855) and Berkeley, California (1866). The independent farmer-preacher system of the Baptists (who were suspicious of the centralized authority of the missionary society structure) increased their denomination's presence in the West and South. The Methodists used itinerant preachers and circuit riders to promote their own religious worldview. Two missions that blur the boundary between "home" and "foreign" were the ones to Oregon and Hawaii. Sponsored by the American Board, these missions, which took place initially in distant territories that were outside the official borders of the United States, laid the groundwork for their later annexation and ultimate statehood. The merits of this interweaving of religion and politics, from the Spanish conquest of the Americas to the twentieth century, is a hotly debated subject. Many non-Christian religious groups, like my own, have been affected by it in negative and sometimes damaging ways. But the importance of the missionary to the work of the Christian Church is beyond dispute.

The figure of the maggid—the itinerant Jewish preacher—appears in Jewish history long before the emergence of the specific term. Some of the earliest rabbis, from nearly two thousand years ago, are depicted in Jewish legends and literature as wandering teachers. Tales I have read about some of the *Hasidei Ashkenaz* show them as beggars and religious vagabonds. But the maggid's position, and the tradition of the traveling preacher, developed more fully during the late Middle Ages. What set the maggid apart from his closest Christian analogue, the missionary, was his function within Jewish society and the content of his message. The maggid was more than a teacher, a pedagogue who transmitted "good news"; he was a social critic, a vehicle for the prophetic voice. He did not proselytize to the heathen, but agitated and inspired the converted. In this role the maggid was often viewed with suspicion by the rabbinic authorities and worked at the margins of Jewish institutional life.

Some scholars have argued that these itinerant preachers, a sort of "nonestablishment intelligentsia," played a key part in the social and religious upheavals in the Jewish world at the end of the seventeenth and during the eighteenth centuries in eastern Europe. "Anyone whose pure-hearted intentions moved him to rove the country to make straight what had become bent," one observer comments, became a peripatetic, self-appointed preacher. The maggid's license came not from the rabbinical courts, but, in his mind, from God. The problem, then as now (many contemporary "spiritual teachers" without any academic credentials often lecture at seminars and retreats), is the inevitable lack of control over mediocrity and charlatanism. There were some preachers who held a semiofficial status in their communities (and in some cases received public funds), but they were not regarded as equals to the rabbi of the town. Because their financial support was so meager, the preachers would be forced to roam the countryside as itinerants—often risking dangerous encounters with brigands and Cossacks—just to eke out a living. Yet for that very reason the maggids were able to reach remote areas that rarely received rabbinic attention.

Owing to the fact that the maggid was in many respects a free agent, he was often quite willing to confront the established leaders over their mistakes or misconduct. This rebelliousness and individualism was linked directly to the growth and popularity of the hasidic movement, which began in the late eighteenth century. Some maggids were also rabbis. Two of the first and greatest hasidic masters (who were the subjects of my rabbinic thesis), Rabbi Yaakov Yosef of Polonnoye and Rabbi Dov Baer of Mezeritch, were both referred to as maggids before and even after they settled into their own communities. But one hasidic master in particular, Rabbi Nachman of Bratslav (1772–1810), seems to embody, through his life and his journeys, the model and spirit of the Jewish itinerant.

Though one of the great rabbis of his era, Nachman showed a certain ambivalence about his vocation, an ambivalence that manifested itself through his many journeys. In Nachman's spiritual worldview, it was not peace and stability, but struggle and movement, that led to inner growth. He once said, "If I were to realize that I stand now at the same place where I stood an hour ago, I would be completely dissatisfied with myself." Nachman was an impressive figure within the hasidic world of his time. He had renown and disciples, but, like many of us today, he could not be still. For Nachman, the spiritual search that was taking place within his soul became externalized; his various journeys throughout the Ukraine and beyond represented not mere wanderlust, but a deep need to work out his inner battles on a concrete playing field. It was this drive that made him take leave of the security of his home, the affection of his family, and the honor of his community and wander through the land. His spiritual mission was as much for himself as it was for others.

From an early age Nachman had an affinity for the outdoors, often going alone to the forests and fields to commune with God. His career as a public figure began with his move to the town of Medvedevka (in the Ukraine) in 1790, where Nachman established a family and, after a period of terrible impoverishment, allowed himself to be supported as a rabbi by a group of local followers. Since the death almost two decades earlier of Rabbi Dov Baer, the Great Maggid of Mezeritch, there had been a dearth of leadership in the hasidic movement, and Nachman now took it upon himself to revitalize a religious community that he felt had atrophied. His approach to Hasidism was not the comforting, lighthearted one of many of his contemporaries, but one that accentuated struggle and soul-searching as the true pathways to inner elevation. It is an approach to living that can serve as an antidote to the warm and fuzzy spirituality of our own era.

In 1798, after a preparatory and somewhat mysterious journey to the city of Kamenets-Podolsk (which was associated with the heretical Frankist movement), Nachman set out for the land of Israel. Perhaps Nachman's descent into the heart of darkness (Kamenets-Podolosk), coupled with his pilgrimage to the Holy Land, was the young rabbi's attempt to purge and purify his soul and make himself ready for the leadership role he believed he was about to assume. Before he could teach, Nachman needed to learn. From Odessa he took a ship to Istanbul and from there to the port city of Haifa. On the surface Nachman acted like a traditional maggid, leading prayers and teaching other Hasidim in the towns of Safed and Tiberias. Yet beneath this exterior an inner journey was also taking place. Nachman made plans to visit Jerusalem, but when Napoleon's forces besieged the Palestinian coastline (they were at war with the Turks and had begun their invasion of Egypt), he was forced to cancel his trip and flee the war zone. By the summer of 1799 he was back in the Ukraine.

Nachman's spiritual development occurred outside the familiarity and comfort of his homeland. This set the pattern for the rest of his life. While his first major journey was the result of his own choice, some were outgrowths of outside pressures. Nachman's difficult and darker model of spirituality could never achieve broad-based popular support, but his attitude and approach made him run afoul of the rest of the hasidic leadership. In 1802, after heated conflicts with other rabbinic authorities, Nachman moved from Zlotopolye (where he and his family had tried to settle) to Bratslav, the town that would become the center of his religious activity for the rest of his life. But his journeys continued. In 1805 he traveled to Shargorad, and in 1807 to the town of Navritch. He writes in a letter: "I have wearied of living in Bratslav, due to the many troubles and misadventures which have befallen me. I shall henceforth be a wanderer from tent to tent, settling nowhere permanently but only sojourning."

His decision to undertake an endless pilgrimage, a voluntary state of exile as a means of self-purification, was cut short by the onset of his wife's tuberculosis. He returned to Bratslav to be with her until her death in the summer of 1807, the same year his own tuberculosis began to develop. His illness seemed to demolish his dream of a life of wandering. Yet even as his physical health deteriorated, Nachman continued to make occasional (though less frequent) rounds of visits to his followers in the towns and villages of the Ukraine. He also made two more major journeys within the country, one to Lemberg in the fall of 1807 (where he spent eight months) and a final one to Uman in 1810. Three days before this last sojourn, a great fire devastated much of Bratslav, destroying Nachman's home. He took it as a sign that he had tarried too long and died in Uman a few months later. While we might view Nachman's journeying as extreme, he clearly embodies a strong impulse within some seekers.

The spiritual hunger that many of us feel today has been present throughout the ages. Yet a large number of those who need religious guidance and comfort are not always the same people sitting in pews and reciting formal prayers. So some of us go to them—*on the road.*

Though it is exciting to teach Torah while traversing the steppes and deserts of Central Asia, or to spread the gospel while paddling in a canoe or riding on horseback, this kind of work also raises profound questions: Why are some of us who have devoted our lives to religion unable to find fulfillment in conventional religious settings? Has our quest to harmonize the call of the wild and the call of faith been the expression of young men and women striving for self-sacrifice or of self-absorbed adrenaline junkies? Who is the real object of our devotion—God, our communities, or ourselves?

At the edge of faith, there is always the danger that altruism and narcissism can become tangled. Yet it is in the heart of this ambiguity that many of us have found our homes.

6 / god undercover

No hymns! Hold the ground gained. Arduous night! The dried blood smokes on my face, and I have nothing behind me but that horrible bush! . . . Spiritual combat is as brutal as the battle of men: but the vision of justice is the pleasure of God alone.

Meanwhile this is the vigil. Welcome then, all the influx of vigor and real tenderness. And, in the dawn, armed with an ardent patience, we shall enter magnificent cities.

ARTHUR RIMBAUD, *A Season in Hell*

"A bullet through the neck," Mike says as he shakes his head and stops for a red light. "Could've been me instead of him." Just an hour earlier the two of us were in Manhattan at a rainy memorial service for a fellow DEA (Drug Enforcement Administration) agent who'd been killed during an undercover operation on Staten Island. Everybody was there: the agent's family, the city's top police brass, bosses from most of the other federal law enforcement agencies. Even Mayor Giuliani showed up for the ceremony. He was the one who, with great solemnity, unveiled the street sign with the agent's name on it, a human life reduced to a sheet of green steel. We drive on in silence. The wipers squeak as they rub back and forth across the windshield. A gym bag on the backseat fills the inside of the car with the smell of sweat. Mike's mustache twitches. He is a tall, muscular man in his late thirties and the father of two children. He shakes his head again. "A bullet through the goddamned neck."

Suddenly the car up ahead of us skids over the median and slams into a stoplight. Glass showers the air like popcorn. The car's purple hood buckles around the thick post. I'm in a hurry, but we can't just drive by. We pull over to the side of the road, stopping a good ten or fifteen yards behind the disabled vehicle. We're not sure how to read the situation. The driver, a white or Hispanic male in his thirties, was driving far too fast for the slick conditions on this suburban street. Mike tells me to keep an eye on the right side of the stalled car as we get out of our car and head toward the driver. Rain drizzles down our trench coats. I notice that Mike's right elbow is slightly cocked, his hand close to the automatic that I know is tucked under his shirt.

I feel an adrenaline rush that reminds me of my first skydiving experience, the moment I stepped out of a Cessna and into an abyss of air. The same uncertainty. The same contraction of my focus. Is the man fleeing the scene of a crime? Is he drunk? Strung out on speed? Does he have a gun or a razor on him? I wonder why I view the man with such suspicion and treat him with so much caution, but I can't help it. That's what they teach you down in Quantico at the Academy. You just never know how anything is going to go down. Within seconds a seemingly innocuous situation can erupt into violence, mayhem, and death. Mike shows the driver his badge and asks the dazed man to step out of the car. He gets out, slowly, and gazes at us. Blood oozes from his forehead. His sweatshirt is torn at the shoulder. He opens his mouth as if to say something, but nothing comes out. The man simply stands there.

Our government-issued Chevy Caprice doesn't have a CB in it, and neither one of us brought a cellular phone. We need to call for an ambulance and get in touch with the local police ASAP (since odds are better than even that this isn't a federal matter). As Mike begins to ask the man some questions, I sprint over to a house across the street in a cul-de-sac of exclusive and luxurious homes. I knock on the front door. A heavy black housekeeper appears at the window, looking weary of her work and wary of me. "Yes?" she asks in a West Indian accent. I reach into my pocket and press my DEA badge against the glass. I feel awkward, as though I'm making use of an authority that I've done nothing to deserve. "Rabbi Niles Goldstein," I say. "I'm a police chaplain. There's a problem at the intersection, and I need to use your phone."

A squad car pulls up within minutes. Mike and I explain to the cop who gets out of it that the two of us are with the DEA and that we'd just driven up from the city when the car in front of us swerved out of control and crashed. He seems confused, even skeptical. For some reason, nobody trusts anybody. The whole scene is charged with suspicion. I've felt it before: the heaviness, the gravity. It's more than mere cautiousness. When faced with a potentially life-threatening situation, the only person you trust is your partner. The driver might reach into his pocket for a gun. The cop's never seen any of us before; he could be incompetent and shoot one of us by mistake. Nobody's on the same side because there *are* no sides. I tell the officer that I'm the assistant rabbi down the street at the temple, and I mention the name of one of his supervisors that I know. He relaxes a bit and says he'll take over from here. As we return to our Chevy I hear a siren in the distance. The ambulance. We leave the cop to sort everything out, still unclear as to whether the driver now leaning with his back against the car is guilty of anything at all other than bad luck and poor timing.

Flanked by tall trees and large homes, we drive just a few hundred feet from the crash along Pinebrook Boulevard. We're in the heart of Westchester, New York's affluent northern suburban region. It's been the venue for my first job as a pulpit rabbi. I've been working here for nearly two years, preaching, marrying, and burying, trying to learn the ropes of the rabbinate week by week. But in serving a congregation more interested in preserving the status quo than in pushing the limits of their moral, intellectual, and spiritual capacities, I'm finding that the idealism I'd brought with me out of rabbinical school is wearing thin.

Mike turns into the driveway, a long and pine-lined lane that leads up a hill to the synagogue complex. The buildings are magnificent pieces of architecture, but the setting is even more spectacular: trees in every direction, rabbits and squirrels darting in and out of shrubs, silence. A far cry from the gritty and dangerous environment that Mike and other federal agents work in all the time. Here I am, the suburban rabbi. My world is circumscribed by baby namings and benedictions. Yet when I'm interacting with men and women who put their lives at risk each and every day, my job feels different. In police work I've found what I'd been craving, an outlet for my energy, an unconventional and exciting context, a community where, at least on the surface, everyone is interested in pushing boundaries and making the world a better place.

We stop in front of the sanctuary. I thank Mike for the ride up from the city and wish him well. He asks me how it feels to have been a cop for the day. I just smile. He can't know how important my chaplaincy work is to me, how vital it is to my own sense of worth—or even to my inner spirituality. Mike says good-bye and drives down the hill, winding around a bend and disappearing in the trees. He's got to head back to his field office on the other side of the Hudson. His squad is working hard to build a case against big-time heroin dealers in Newburgh. It's time for me to go to work, too. Our youth group is holding a dance tonight that I have to chaperone. I take off my trench coat and put on my yarmulke.

I have to admit the whole thing is a bit ironic. For a young man who has been arrested and jailed by the NYPD and interrogated by the KGB, becoming a police chaplain does not seem particularly logical. It started about six years ago. As I sat at a downtown bar nursing a Guinness, three burly men walked through the front door, looked around, then approached me and said, "You the rabbi?" These men were special agents from the Federal Law Enforcement Officers Association, the umbrella group for agents from the FBI, DEA, ATF, Secret Service, and all the other federal law enforcement agencies in New York and around the country. FLEOA was looking for a new national Jewish chaplain. My interview lasted a couple of hours. They asked me questions that had never been posed to me before, always looking me in the eyes to weigh my reaction. The oldest agent, an enormous U.S. marshal in his fifties, did most of the questioning:

"Know anything about cop culture?"

"Ever seen a gunshot wound?"

"How would you handle a crisis situation?"

My answers seemed to satisfy them, as did the fact that I'd gone through boot camp for the U.S. Army's chaplaincy program. After they found out that I had a black belt in karate, one of them started calling me "Rabbicop." I felt at ease and disarmed, as if I were just drinking beer with some old buddies instead of being questioned by cops. Then I'd catch sight of one of their gun holsters. I was offered the position, provided I passed a standard security clearance. Since my arrest several years earlier had not led to a conviction, it did not affect my appointment as a chaplain.

Entering the world of cops and criminals is not a common career move for a rabbi, but the fundamental mission of law enforcement—the pursuit of justice—seemed to mesh perfectly with one of the central tenets of my faith. The prophet Isaiah declares: "Justice, justice shall you pursue!" I've seen that charge before the eyes of scores of agents and cops. Not that there aren't some bad ones. There are. But never before had I met so many individuals into whose hands I would entrust my life.

For centuries the military has recognized the value of having clergy among its troops. Even in the Bible, from the high priest

Aaron standing watch over desert battlefields to Joshua's priests blowing rams' horns at the walls of Jericho, the active presence of religious figures in life-threatening situations was indispensable. For morale, religious officiation, and spiritual guidance, there was simply no substitute. Yet the position of law enforcement chaplain, certainly for the various federal agencies, is a relatively new one. Because of this fact our roles aren't always clearly defined. Some of our responsibilities vary not only from agency to agency, but frequently even within field offices. Rather than viewing this ambiguity as a hurdle, I've treated it as an opportunity.

There's no other congregation I know of where a bar stool or a squad car can become a pulpit. The trick to any successful ministry is to meet people where they are—and cops tend to congregate in some pretty dark places. I've counseled agents in pubs and discussed marital problems in interrogation rooms. My work is unpredictable. I wear a beeper. When an agent's in trouble (which could mean anything from being involved in a shooting to contemplating suicide) it goes off. Sometimes an agent just wants to meet for a beer and schmooze. These men and women tend to keep their problems to themselves. They're afraid department shrinks will inform on them to their supervisors. Law enforcement officers as a whole are a pretty distrustful bunch and often have a dim view of human nature and the world—they deal with society's underbelly on a daily basis. They've seen and heard it all. Losing faith in the benevolence of God is an occupational hazard.

Though many of my duties are fairly straightforward (being on call for emergencies, counseling agents, officiating at memorials and religious ceremonies), sometimes I feel as if I'm making up my job as I go along. This has its advantages. With few institutional precedents or models, I've tried to push the boundaries of police chaplaincy as much as possible. I didn't want to simply hear about the work of the agents I served—I wanted to *live* some of it. After a short time working as a chaplain for the DEA's New York field division, I met with its special agent in charge. I told him I needed to spend time with agents in the field. If one of my responsibilities as a chaplain was to help them with their stresses from the job, then I had to experience their work environment. He agreed and arranged for me to go with a pair of agents into Washington Heights and the South Bronx, two of the city's most violent and drug-infested areas.

"Wear your civvies," they told me over the phone. "Jeans and sneakers." That was fine with me. I always looked forward to taking off the jacket-and-tie uniform of a conventional rabbi. The agents met me in front of my apartment in Park Slope, Brooklyn. They didn't honk—they signaled me with a piercing, quick blast from their siren. I introduced myself as I entered their conspicuously anonymous blue Chevy Caprice: "Call me Niles," I said. One of the agents, Rob, was a young Jewish guy. The other, John, was a slightly older Catholic who'd been a cop before he joined the DEA. They couldn't get over the fact that I was a rabbi yet looked and behaved so much as they did. But I wasn't the only one who defied a stereotype. The three of us looked more as though we were on our way to Yankee Stadium than heading off to work. I bought us all some coffee before we crossed the Brooklyn Bridge into Manhattan and headed north up the FDR Drive toward Washington Heights.

I'd never seen so many beeper and electronics stores in my life. Many of them, I learned, were front businesses for drug dealers. Some of them had been raided already. The dealers often had better surveillance systems in their buildings than the police—videocameras picked up raids before they could even happen. Dozens of teenagers were "hanging out" around public telephones, waiting for calls or pages. Most everyone seemed to know that we were cops (which probably wasn't too difficult in our car and in the largely black Dominican community). As we turned down one street known for drug exchanges, we saw groups of young men congregating on the stoops of run-down brownstones. Their eyes followed us. There was hatred in them. Although I was with federal agents who had badges and guns, my blood ran cold.

"The vast majority of people who live in Washington Heights are law-abiding citizens," said John, picking up on my anxiousness.

"It's the dirtbags who turn this place into a battleground," Rob chimed in. "Makes me sick, these little kids growing up with all this garbage around them."

Drug-dealing, coupled with recent tensions between residents and the NYPD, had made the place one of New York's most troubled and sensitive areas. The agents told me about their frustrations with the criminal justice system, about how little (if any) time behind bars any of the dealers wound up serving before they were back on the streets. Even when one was put away, another dealer would take his place the next day. There was constant—and often deadly—jockeying for position. Their work, the agents said, was endless and maddening, without any real appreciation from the outside or apparent benefit to the neighborhood.

On another day we drove through sections of the South Bronx, which didn't feel much safer. They looked as if they'd been strafed by gunfire. I saw a lot of people going about their everyday lives, but I also saw dealers, junkies, and prostitutes. It was grim. A decade ago, the agents told me, the main drugs on the street were depressants, like heroin and marijuana. Now they were stimulants like crack cocaine and methamphetamines. The whole atmosphere had changed for the worse. Violence had increased exponentially. Weapons were everywhere. Crack and crystal meth were ripping the guts out of entire neighborhoods.

John proceeded to tell me about an arrest that went bad. Two years earlier he and two other DEA agents had tried to serve a warrant in Brooklyn. The three of them were standing shoulder to shoulder on the front steps of a dilapidated building when the suspect opened the door and shot at them from point-blank range. John's partner at the time took a bullet in the arm. Fearing for their lives, John returned fire and killed the man. Within hours, before he even had time to reflect on what had just happened, he was ordered to turn in his weapon.

"It's like asking a rabbi to turn in his Torah," John explained to me. "Or telling a priest he can no longer celebrate mass."

After the incident John was given a Department of Justice handbook on postshooting trauma and told to read it while they began an investigation to see if it was a "good" shooting. John was suspended from most of his responsibilities in the field. The coldness and formality of the process did nothing to alleviate his feelings of guilt.

"I was a textbook case," he continued. "All the classic symptoms. My sleep grew erratic, I became more and more withdrawn, and for three months I had this recurring nightmare where I'd be walking through Central Park and I'd come across that same guy. We'd shoot at each other until I woke up in a cold sweat."

In the seminary they teach you how to comfort those who are in mourning—not those who have been in combat. When I started as a chaplain, I was struck by the contrast between the ethereality of religion (with its beliefs, rituals, and liturgies) and the grittiness of police work. I saw my job as trying to bridge these two worlds. But I didn't know what to say to John. For several minutes all I could do was listen. Rob just stared out the window. Finally I asked John if he had approached anyone for help. Like many others I've encountered in law enforcement, he hadn't. For him this was part of the job, something he would simply have to work through on his own.

"My wife wanted me to quit," he added. "I couldn't. I liked being a cop." John looked down at the steering wheel. "I'm convinced that the shooting partly led to our divorce."

We drove past a group of teenagers waiting near a public telephone. They watched us coldly until we passed. I asked John how his work had affected his spiritual life, if confronting the darker side of human nature had begun to beat down his soul.

"You're so busy trying to chase down the bad guys that you don't have time to ask yourself the big questions," he said. "Until you're in a shooting. Then all that occupies your mind is how fragile and temporary everything is. You think about taking care of your family. About what comes next, whether or not this is the end of the line."

John went on to tell me that he was cleared in the investigation and put back on the street. His days were again marked by crack, hookers, and automatic weapons. Now he was just trying to put the pieces of his life back together.

"It can be pretty tough working in an environment like this," Rob said. "Sometimes it makes you angry."

"Or lose faith," added John. "So tell us, rabbi, where is God in all this?"

I'd heard the question many times before in different contexts. This time it felt different. More raw. It was difficult—even for me as a clergyman—to find meaning or experience holiness in an atmosphere of such desperation and potential violence. I wasn't sure how to answer him. I was also unsure as to what the agent was *really* asking. Was he looking for a fancy theological explanation of the problem of evil? Or did he simply want to air his inner conflict to someone who understood his world and who'd take his dilemma as seriously as he took it? G-men need God just as much as anybody else. Maybe even more so. They need spiritual counselors to listen to their problems, struggles, and frustrations. What they don't need is someone to preach at them from a pulpit in the heavens.

"I don't know for certain," I answered. "Maybe in the embrace of a partner whose life you've saved. I guess it depends on how hard you're willing to look."

Many of today's "spirituality" teachers offer game plans and formulas for finding God in our lives. You don't have that luxury in law enforcement work. In the face of contract killings, gang warfare, and the ravages of smack, you won't find God out in the open. You have to look undercover, in the shadows. Nothing's clean in Copland. That is the challenge of the agents I serve. As their chaplain, it's mine, too. Everything there, even spirituality, is dirty business. If God is everywhere and with us at all times—if God is truly *God*—then we should be able to discover the divine in the darkness as well as in the light. For those of us whose daily lives draw us into some of those murkier regions, we just have to strain our eyes a little more.

That darkness is not limited just to the world of law enforcement. Life itself can often be bleak and grim. We are constantly bombarded, through the various media as well as our own experiences, with images not only of crime, but of deep human suffering. Stories and TV clips of torture, rape, mutilation, and genocide in places like Rwanda and Bosnia numb our sensitivities and make murders in Denver or Houston seem commonplace, even acceptable. Since evil and misery seem to be constants of the human condition, how can there be a God? And if there is a God, how can we have a meaningful relationship with a being who permits such ugliness and pain to be a part of creation and who seems so detached and far away? Two powerful and creative religious thinkers, Menahem Mendel of Kotsk (1787–1859) and Søren Kierkegaard (1813–1855), offer fascinating and somewhat similar explanations to these profound existential questions.

Menahem Mendel was born near Lublin, Poland. He spent much of his youth studying with two of the Hasidic masters of his time, Yaakov Yitzhak ha-Hozeh ("the Seer") of Lublin and Yaakov Yitzhak ("the Holy Jew") of Pshyskhe, and later with Simha Bunam of Pshyskhe, whom he succeeded, living first in Tomashov and then in Kotsk until his death at the age of seventy-two. Menahem Mendel was a controversial figure within the hasidic movement. While the founder of Hasidism, the Baal Shem Tov, emphasized joy and love in his spirituality, Menahem Mendel advocated constant combat against egocentricity as the path toward inner fulfillment. While the Baal Shem Tov spoke of the immanent presence of God in the world, Menahem Mendel taught that a great gap separated God from the world. In his intellectual departure from the religious worldview of Hasidism's founder, Menahem Mendel was similar to Dov Baer of Mezeritch. But whereas the latter became a key player in the unfolding of the movement, Menahem Mendel remained a disquieting figure at the fringe of his community. He was interested in reaching not the masses, but the few, the select. His goal was not to gather disciples, but to uncover the Truth, and for the Kotsker rebbe Truth was buried away from human view, as if in a grave.

Menahem Mendel never committed his thoughts to writing. Luckily for us, his son-in-law wrote about his life, and his followers, though relatively few in number, recorded the sayings, aphorisms, and parables of their master. There is one parable in particular that captures the essence of Menahem Mendel's spiritual vision as well as his attitude toward human life. He explains that all souls descend a ladder from heaven down to our world, a different ladder for each soul. Once they have arrived, the ladder is removed. In time they are commanded to ascend back to heaven. Some despair and do not even try to ascend because their ladder is gone. Others jump up and fall, again and again, until they too give up. But a few souls refuse to surrender, despite the apparent futility of leaping and crashing back down to earth. We must do what God asks of us, they say, no matter the consequence of our actions or the impossibility of our task. They leap and leap, and plummet over and over to the ground, until in an act of mercy God draws them up to heaven.

For the Kotsker rebbe, it is by never giving up, even in the face of what seems like utter futility, that redemption comes to human beings. When we "leap" toward God, we are aiming not for the known, but the *un*known. It is an act of faith. There is no assurance that we will not be wounded (or worse) through our efforts. But human effort alone is not sufficient to bring about our redemption. For that we need divine aid, the gift of grace. The ladder that connected our primordial souls to God no longer exists. A chasm divides us from God, an abyss of egocentricity and human limitation. The concerns and senses that root us to the physical world hinder our vision of the world of the spirit; the reason that produces scientific knowledge is unable to fathom a transcendent God, a God who transcends reason itself. As the Kotsker said, "A God whom any dirty, little man could understand I could not believe in."

Faith is more than a challenge. It is pain. For God's reality is inextricably linked to God's absence, the void of separation we feel in our lives. *That* is Menahem Mendel's proof for the existence of God—not empirical evidence or rational demonstration. But this absence is part illusory. An ancient midrash (rabbinic story) that seemed to especially captivate the Kotsker, and one that he taught to his students, conveys this idea. A man once wandered from city to city and came upon a palace that was engulfed in flames. Since no one seemed to be present and trying to put out the fire, he wondered to himself: Could it be that this palace has no lord? But suddenly a figure, whom he could barely discern through the smoke, looked down on him from one of the windows and said, "I am the lord of this palace."

The Kotsker interpreted this midrash as a metaphor for God's relationship to creation. When we look at our world we see beauty and joy, but we also see war, starvation, homelessness, disease, suffering. Our palace is aflame. And when we look for God, when we search for a Creator to put an end to the horrors of creation, we come up empty-handed. God seems absent. But this is a half-truth. While God may transcend the world, God is still, paradoxically, the "lord of the palace." God suffers with us, in the trenches, in the heart of the flames. Though we might not know with absolute certainty that our palace has a Master (or that we possess a special ladder that unites the two of us directly), and though it is our task, and ours alone, to look for the Master's presence despite the heat, fire, and smoke (or to leap for heaven despite the apparent futility of our efforts), God is with us, the gift of our tenaciousness, the prize of our indomitable will. God is present because God *has* to be.

God is the answer to our needs, our yearnings. But first we must give voice to them. In another parable, the Kotsker illustrates this point. One day the prophet Elijah met a hunter in the wilderness. He asked the hunter why he was living alone in the wilderness without the Torah or its commandments. The man answered by saying, "Because I could never find the gate that leads to the presence of God."

"You were certainly not born a hunter," Elijah responded. "So from whom did you learn to follow this calling?"

"My need taught me," answered the hunter.

Then the prophet said: "And had your need been equally great because you had lost your way far from God, do you think it would have failed to show you the way to Him?"

Through this parable, Menahem Mendel seems to be showing us that God's presence has less to do with God's external reality than with our inner lives. We must *want* God. This gives humanity much more power than might be apparent. God is there, waiting for us. But if we give up too easily, if we don't make a serious effort to find God, we will remain lost in a spiritual wilderness. The Kotsker asks elsewhere: "Where is God? In the place where He is given entry." He also says, "One who does not see the Omnipresent in every place will not see Him in any place." Whether or not God is an active part of our lives is up to us. If we cannot find God, it is not because we are looking in the wrong places, but because we are not looking hard enough. If the hunter put as much intensity into tracking down God as he does into chasing wild animals, he would find far more than food.

The Kotsker comments on the following text from the Talmud: "When Nebuchadnezzer, the mighty king of Babylonia, wanted to sing praises to God, an angel came and slapped him in the face." Menahem Mendel asks: "Why did the king deserve to be slapped, if his intention was to sing God's praises?" He responds in God's voice: "You want to sing praises while you are wearing a crown? Let me hear how you praise Me after having been slapped in the face!" The paradox of a transcendent deity is that even as God is hidden from the world, God is present everywhere in it. Not just in light, but in darkness. Not just in the raptures of joy, but in the heart of pain. It is too easy to have faith when life is good. Meaningful faith occurs when we disregard ourselves, when we believe in God despite our own hardship and suffering.

The Bible teaches us, "Even the darkness is not too dark for You." (Psalms 139:12) The Kotsker interprets this verse to mean that when we come to understand that everything in our world, including its darker aspects, derives from God, we begin to realize that much of what we perceive as "bad" is, from the divine perspective, simply another piece of the sacred whole. Like the tiny dots that constitute Georges Seurat's famous painting, *A Sunday Afternoon on the Island of La Grande Jatte,* those experiences in our lives that up close seem so uncomfortable, anarchic, and disorienting are, from a distance, actually essential components of a beautiful and harmonious creation. That which appears as darkness to us may very well be the beacon to our redemption.

About two decades before his death, for reasons that are not altogether clear, Menahem Mendel withdrew from the world. He locked himself in a room near the house of study where his disciples would learn. Food was passed to him through a window, and he was rarely seen by anyone but his closest friends or family members. A legend has the aged rabbi walk in one day on his students, who were gathered in worship. As they prayed, oblivious of his presence, he shouted at them: "Liars! You're all liars!" Then he retreated to the seclusion of his room. For the Kotsker, the key to spirituality is not pietistic practice or divine disclosure, but what happens within ourselves. God is ultimately beyond us. Our task is to be true to our humanity, to uncover our hearts and let them lead the way toward God. How do we accomplish this goal? The Kotsker says, "It is sufficient for a person to unlock in his heart a tiny opening, as the point of a needle, provided that he will feel a prick in his heart, as a burning in living flesh, and not as a needle thrust into dead meat."

The relationship between God and humanity is often expressed these days through the use of soothing metaphors and images. One such example is light, and lines like "My soul was caressed by a divine light" would not be out of place in many of the current spirituality books and testimonials. But to religious thinkers like the Kotsker, a better image for conveying this dynamic is that of *fire.* Few things in our world are as intangible and ungraspable as a flame. Its external form is too fluid to define, and its inner substance is too hot to touch. Fire can give us warmth and comfort, but it can also burn us and cause great pain. It is an indispensable part of human life, yet it is still inaccessible. Fire has a transcendent quality. Søren Kierkegaard, a Christian contemporary of the Kotsker's, thought of God—and our relationship to God—in similar ways.

Kierkegaard was born in 1813 in Copenhagen, the youngest child of a wealthy and devout Lutheran father. His childhood was not a happy one, and melancholy would continue to plague his soul (and become manifest in much of his writing) throughout his life. The Danish philosopher and theologian began his studies at Copenhagen University in 1830. At first he lived a life of profligacy and epicurean self-indulgence, dressing in expensive clothes, lounging in cafés and taverns, and debauching about town with his friends. But then something happened that made Kierkegaard shift his course dramatically. Despite his years of carousing and secular living, and perhaps because of his stern Lutheran upbringing, Kierkegaard had still made intermittent forays into the world of organized religion and prayer. Nothing much happened for him in church. Yet on the morning of May 18, 1838, he underwent a deep spiritual experience that filled him with "a joy which cools and refreshes us like a breath of wind, a wave of air, from the trade wind which blows from the plains of Mamre to the everlasting habitations." We do not know what caused this experience, but from that morning on Kierkegaard's life would never be the same. As he wrote soon after this transformative event, "I mean to labor to achieve a far more inward relation to Christianity; hitherto I have fought for its truth while in a sense standing outside it."

Before he could turn to this task, there were some broken pieces in Kierkegaard's life that he wanted to try to make whole. His relationship with his father, Michael Pedersen Kierkegaard, was strained. Although it was his father who had encouraged him to pursue theological studies at the university, Kierkegaard held him responsible for two profound and (especially to his son) disturbing religious transgressions. According to biographers, in his youth Michael Kierkegaard was a shepherd who lived in dire poverty. Enraged by his terrible lot, he attacked heaven and once even cursed

God. Michael carried the feeling of guilt with him to the end, and it became his son Søren's burden as well. As a young adult, Kierkegaard also learned from his father of another sin. This one had been kept a secret from him for his entire life, and it now struck him as a "great earthquake": Søren had been conceived out of wedlock, his father having married his maid (Søren's mother) after the death of his first wife, when the maid was in her fourth month of pregnancy. After his religious conversion, Søren was able to forgive and become reconciled with his father, who died just three months later.

Kierkegaard had yet another broken piece in his life—loneliness—that he wanted to make whole. In 1840 he fell in love with and became engaged to a seventeen-year-old girl, Regine Olsen. But he broke off the engagement thirteen months later. This decision, which was rooted in his feeling that marriage was ultimately irreconcilable with his calling to be a religious writer, haunted him for the rest of his life. That which he yearned for most could not be. Years later, a few days before his death, Kierkegaard confided to a close friend: "I am depressed. Like Paul, I had my 'thorn in the flesh'; so that I was unable to enter into the usual relations of life and I therefore concluded that my task was extraordinary; and I tried to carry it out as best I could; I was the toy of providence which produced me and I was to be used; and then crash! and providence stretched out its hand and took me into the ark; that is always the life and fate of the extraordinary messenger." At the very end, looking back over the whole of his life, Kierkegaard laments but accepts the fact that his had been a faith that drove him to the edge.

In 1841, after his relationship with Regine had ended, he wrote in his journal: "Either you throw yourself into the wildest kind of life—or else become absolutely religious, but it will be different from the parson's mixture." He chose the latter, though he knew from the beginning that his path would be far different (and probably that it would be much more at the margins of the established church) than that of the conventional religious authorities of his time. Kierkegaard finished his degree and entered a period of intense literary fruition, publishing eight books between 1843 and 1846. Yet devoting one's life to God can burn. Kierkegaard became a well-known figure in Copenhagen, and in 1846 the *Corsair* (a satirical newspaper) lampooned him in a series of articles and cartoons. The pieces, which were written by a former friend and drinking companion from his university years, mocked Kierkegaard's dress, ridiculed his somber personality, and made fun of his broken engagement. Too afraid of the paper themselves, none of his friends came to his defense. Judging by his journal entries, this torturous episode helped to shape Kierkegaard's self-perception and worldview. Suffering was not a punishment for sins, but a prerequisite to becoming a servant of God in a world where God's presence is absent and which loathes those—like himself—who try to walk the true spiritual path.

This theological position, among others, put Kierkegaard at odds with the official church and its prelates, including his own brother (who was a bishop). But Kierkegaard would not accept criticism from those he did not respect. In his book *Attack upon "Christendom,"* Kierkegaard argues that the bourgeois Christians of his time had turned Christianity into a sweet faith of sentimental love, a religion fit for little more than children. He claims that the church had made Christianity too comfortable and easy in its attempts to be accepted by the masses, going so far as to write that God should take *back* the New Testament, since no one in his day could handle it properly. Kierkegaard even tried to dissuade congregants from crossing the church threshold. As a result of his uncompromising and relentless attacks on mainstream Christianity, Kierkegaard was treated in his own time as a pariah and a marginal figure not worth paying attention to, and his religious writing was largely ignored.

At the heart of Kierkegaard's belief system is a transcendent God, a God who, like a burning flame, is untouchable, elusive, inaccessible. The thrust of post-Renaissance thought had been on a concept of God immanent in history and human experience. Hegel was one of the most influential thinkers in this area, arguing that God (or the "Infinite Spirit") was not distinct from the finite world, but manifested in it. To Kierkegaard this notion was anathema. He claims that there is a "deep gulf of qualitative difference" between human beings and God. Humanity belongs in the sphere of existence, and God, the divine Other, belongs in the sphere of the infinite and the eternal, independent of the world. We are not different from God just in terms of capacities (such as power or life span), but in kind. Only an indirect relationship with divinity is possible. While philosophy tries to reduce religious matters into clear and tangible knowledge, Kierkegaard writes that true religion is irreducible, "not a doctrine, but an existential contradiction." It is not enough for a spiritual person to philosophize about the categories of faith: God, the soul, sin, suffering. One must *live* in them, along with the tension and discomfort that they necessarily engender.

It is in the arena of rationality that this gulf of difference is most pronounced. For Kierkegaard, the faculty of reason is not capable of a direct apprehension of God, of grasping "what is absolutely different from itself." The paradox of thought is that it wants "to discover something that thought itself cannot think." In Kierkegaard's view, the unknown that reason collides with as it strives for knowledge is none other than God. It may not be known or knowable, but it is real, it exists. Our collision with this absolute frontier does not satisfy the passion of our understanding. When thought is drawn to and searches for its outer limit, it encounters something that it does not comprehend. God is "the frontier that is continually arrived at" but never crossed, the incentive of our reason as well as its deepest torment. Our relationship with God transcends our conceptualization of God, and it is not an easy dynamic. Kierkegaard's God, like the Kotsker's, is "hidden." To try to define God is to distance ourselves from the divine, to stand outside the relationship and to treat God not as a partner, but as a thing, an idol. As Kierkegaard writes in one of his poems, "Father in Heaven! You are incomprehensible in Your creation; You live far off in a light which no one can penetrate, and if we recognize You in Your providence, our knowledge is feeble and veils Your splendor."

Faith involves risk, for it is rooted in the conflict between the boundless passion of the believer and the stark wall of objective uncertainty. Faith begins where thought ends. Since the object of faith is an absolute paradox, faith is an offense to the mind, an affront to our yearning for intellectual apprehension. Faith must be an act of the *will*, the product not of rational demonstration, but of an existential "leap" toward the unknown. Kierkegaard argues that faith needs room to "venture," to make the passionate, nonrational leap whereby the individual comes to believe. This room derives from uncertainty, which, paradoxically, "tortures forth the passionate certainty of faith" in God. But faith is not a permanent state, a comfortable and sustained place of rest. It is a constant and painful struggle, a battle, the ultimate tension. Faith must be renewed continually, over and over, like the actions of the figures who leap for heaven in the Kotsker's dramatic parable on life.

If a gulf separates and hides God from humanity, how does revelation take place? It is up to us, not God, to bridge the abyss. Direct revelation destroys the uncertainty that drives human beings to make the leap of faith and therefore stunts spiritual growth. True revelation occurs indirectly, not in colorful theophanies, but in the individual's inward and ethical self-development. As we reach for (and reveal ourselves to) God, God comes to be revealed to us. Only through faith do we, like Job, learn to see God everywhere and in all things. That includes adversity and pain, even horror. The person of faith, the individual who has brushed up against infinite possibility, is better equipped to face reality and knows that life is not always joyful and secure, that "terror, perdition, annihilation dwell next door." For the believer, the mark of God's presence is God's apparent absence. The more that outward appearances (such as brutality, injustice, or intellectual uncertainty) seem to exclude the possibility of a God, the more God is actually present for the person with faith. And our battle to achieve that faith must take place, "not fantastically in the church," but out in the real world, the world of struggle and suffering, the world where God really lives, but lives undercover.

By the time of his death in 1855 Kierkegaard had written thirty books, as well as kept a long and detailed journal he had begun when he was twenty. As he lay on his deathbed in a hospital, his brother, the bishop, tried to visit him. Kierkegaard would not see him. He had been in a state of war with the church for two decades, and during his last days he expressed to a friend, through an analogy, just how dire and painful this war had been to him. "In a wildboar hunt," Kierkegaard said, "the huntsman has a hound, a picked animal; they know what will happen; the wildboar will be thrown, but it kills the hound that catches it." Earlier, in his journal, he had written that the ultimate purpose of all his work could be summed up in a single thought: "to wound from behind." Kierkegaard viewed himself as the hound of heaven, a prophetic voice. If he had wounded (or even "killed") religion by sacrificing his personal life, it was only to purge religion of its vapidity, to lay the groundwork for a new and more passionate faith.

If God doesn't exist in the shadows as well as in the light, then God doesn't exist. The Kotsker and Kierkegaard make this point repeatedly in their teachings, and I have come to that conclusion myself through my work as a police chaplain. It is an idea that is also embedded deeply in scripture. In return for all he has done for his people and all he has given up for his God, Moses pleads with God in

the book of Exodus: "Pray let me see your *kavod*." God treats Moses's request to see the *kavod* (usually translated as "glory") as a desire to see God's face and denies it: "You cannot see My face, for no human can see Me and live." Instead God tells him that when the divine presence passes by, God will place Moses in the cleft of a rock and screen him with God's hand, for "you shall see My back, but My face shall not be seen."

When I first read these verses, Goya's famous painting *The Colossus* entered into my mind. I'd seen it in Madrid: towering over and turned away from fleeing humans and beasts stands a giant, poised for battle, with an enormous, muscular back. The relationship between the masses below and the giant above is ambiguous; what is clear is that it is not a relationship of equals. Is the colossus protecting them from some invisible danger? Or is he himself instilling fear and trembling in them? A transcendent God can have a similar effect on us. Though we may want to see God on our own terms—unobscured and out in the light—the message of tradition seems to be that God's back is all any of us (including Moses) can hope to see. God *has* no face. The only kind of knowledge about the divine we should expect will be limited and indirect. We can know *that* God is, but never *who* God is. God's existence and sheer reality (God's "back"), not God's true nature and ungraspable *kavod* (God's "face"), belong to the domain of human experience. Intimate knowledge of God is beyond our ability in this life—but perhaps not in the life to come. As Paul writes in Corinthians I, "Now we see through a glass, darkly; but then face-to-face."

7 / midnight sun

In the woods, we return to reason and faith. There I feel that nothing can befall me in life—no disgrace, no calamity (leaving me my eyes), which nature cannot repair. Standing on the bare ground—my head bathed by the blithe air and uplifted into infinite space—all mean egotism vanishes. I become a transparent eyeball; I am nothing; I see all; the currents of the Universal Being circulate through me; I am part or parcel of God. I am the lover of uncontained and immortal beauty. In the wilderness, I find something more dear and connate than in streets or villages. In the tranquil landscape, and especially in the distant line of the horizon, man beholds somewhat as beautiful as his own nature.

RALPH WALDO EMERSON, *Nature*

After my first year as a rabbi, as well as my first experiences working in the professional Jewish world, I felt a deep need to return to Alaska. I wanted to reignite the spark that had originally propelled me into rabbinical school with so much zeal and idealism. As a young rabbi I had longed for a religious community that was bursting with pride, joy, passion, and vitality, that held as its eternal mandate the loving commitment to a sacred covenant between its members and God. What I discovered was something else: a cult of woe, a reactionary community that seemed to be obsessed with its own degeneration, with intermarriage, assimilation, anti-Semitism, and the Holocaust. I was losing my faith.

I had to get away, to return to a place where I could once again find inspiration for my soul. I made arrangements to fly to Fair-

banks, where I had worked for a summer three years before as the student rabbi for the town's Jewish community. My friend Dave had been working up there as an environmentalist and wilderness guide and raised dogs on the side. We decided to meet in the early spring for a dogsledding adventure north of the Arctic Circle, our second mushing trip together. I spent most of March trying to find the appropriate gear in Manhattan for a trip to the Last Frontier, but by the end of the month I had everything pieced together and I'd arrived in Fairbanks. Dave met me at the airport in his rusty shambles of a truck, and within fifteen minutes we were back at his cabin, unloading the sleds from the vehicle's roof and hooking up our dogs to their tug lines for a practice run through the dark and icy night.

It had been two years since I'd last stood on a dogsled. On our first trip, a five-day foray into a starkly beautiful area known as the White Mountains, everything was a challenge for me: putting harnesses on the team, learning the verbal commands for my lead dogs, making turns without falling off the sled into the snow. This time most of it came back to me within minutes. It was night, but because I had to be back in New York the following week, we didn't have much time to wait for me to regain my bearings. It had been warm that past week, so by the time we got onto the trails the daytime melt had frozen and they were rock hard. We wore headlamps to make our way through the darkness. Whenever the dogs looked back toward me, their eyes flashed in the beams like blue moons. It took us just half an hour to mush around the outskirts of Fairbanks to Hidden Hill, a small Quaker community where some of Dave's friends lived. They served us fresh salmon and homemade pumpkin pie.

Sated from my meal and anxious to get back to the dogs resting outside, I thanked our hosts and put on my boots. The air that had stung my face during our run to Hidden Hill felt refreshing as I walked out of the cabin. (If you dressed warmly enough, the cold months in the Alaskan interior were bearable—unless you had to deal with wind.) Stars filled the sky, an immense swath of blackness. It was a different world from New York. It seemed a more *real* world. A dozen pairs of eyes stared at me silently. My feet crunched into the snow as I walked toward our sleds. Suddenly the dogs erupted into a frenzy of barking and lunging. The vague animal forms grew clearer as my vision adjusted to the night. There were our two teams, thrashing and howling in wild expectation of the trail. I recognized only a few of them from our last trip; Dave had borrowed several of these new dogs for me from a friend.

The first time I saw sled dogs I was struck by their lack of size. From the photographs I had seen of them in magazines and newspapers, I had expected them to be quite large. But up close, except for their thickened fur and tight, powerful musculature, they looked like house pets. Our dogs were mongrels, mixtures of Alaskan malamutes and Siberian huskies. Most were no more than fifty or sixty pounds. Each dog has a different role to play on the team. The biggest and strongest ones—the wheel dogs—are positioned closest to the sled. Their job is to pull. My wheel dogs were named Cody (Dave's personal favorite, who doubled as a house dog) and Smiley (whom we eventually started calling "Jar Head" because he had the temperament of a marine). Next in line are the swing dogs. They make up the main body of the team, especially if it is a large race team, like the ones used in the Iditarod or the Yukon Quest. All these animals have to do is follow the dogs in front of them. Brown and Riley were my swing dogs. Finally, at the head of the team and most distant from the sled, are the lead dogs. Sometimes a musher uses a single dog for this role; often he or she uses two. These dogs have to be smart, since they are the ones who respond to the musher's commands (go, stop, turn left, turn right, and so on) and who can make or break a team. Mine were named Masai and Oosik.

To prevent the energetic dogs from racing off with our empty and light sleds while we were eating inside the cabin, we had turned the sleds on their sides and secured their ice hooks (anchors) into the frozen snow. Dave and I needed a few minutes to untangle some members of our teams who had crossed tug lines with each other. Then, after first making sure that both of us were safely behind our sleds, we simultaneously turned our sleds upright, pulled the hooks from the ice, and shouted "Haw!" to our lead dogs. The command was superfluous. The teams bolted down the trail the instant they heard the ice hooks being removed. Mushing through a cold Alaskan night was unlike anything I had ever experienced. The sensation itself, similar to skiing or surfing, is not what is remarkable. It is the *scene.* You stand alone on a sled in darkness. Other than your headlamp, only the moon lights your way through the woods and over the streams and rivers. Frigid wind blasts your face. A team of animals, silenced by their exertions, pulls you forward over snow and ice with a focus that makes it seem as if nothing in the world but running ultimately matters to them. Little matters to you, either, but the moment.

The following day, while Dave took care of some last-minute errands related to our sleds and camping gear, I drove around Fairbanks buying food for our trip. Dave had prepared two long lists for me, one for us and the other for the dogs. First I went to the supermarket. I got the basics for a cold weather journey: rice, beans, butter, cheese, meat (for him), fish (for me), and crackers that were hard enough to survive the rough and tumble of the trail. We would have to pack all of it, labeled by type of meal, tightly into our sleds. They would double as freezers. Liquor was a trickier issue. Beer did not have enough alcohol content to hold its liquid form, so unless we wanted to drink ice we had to purchase harder stuff. The spirit we settled on for our Arctic excursion was rum. When I was finished gathering our supplies, I concentrated on our teams. Dog food had never seemed so complicated. Because of all the energy the dogs would burn during the trip, Dave spelled out very carefully what I needed to buy in order to replenish them: beef fat (for a quick jolt of energy), dry dog food (to be mixed with warm water to help rehydrate them), and several fifty-pound sacks of ground and compressed meat with a bold label on them that read CONDEMNED CHICKEN CARCASSES: NOT FIT FOR HUMAN CONSUMPTION.

After my tasks were completed, I had a couple of spare hours to see some of my former congregants. I'd been in touch by telephone with a few of them over the past three years. I visited Leah and Mike, who proudly showed me their new house—and I used a flush toilet for what I knew would be the last time in a week. I also met with Richard and Margot, who proudly gave me a tour of the very first synagogue the Jews of Fairbanks had owned, which they had just bought (when I lived there in 1992, we held our Sabbath services in the chapel at Fort Wainwright, the town's sprawling army base). Richard wept as he walked me through the building. While it was nice to catch up with old friends, seeing everybody again felt somewhat strange. The context was completely different. In my time of need, I wasn't turning to the Jewish community for spiritual revitalization. I was turning to the wilderness.

That evening it took three hours for Dave and me to pack all our gear and supplies into the two sleds, each of which was a good eight feet in length. We jammed the least frequently used items (such as the tent) near the front, placed the heaviest items (like our stove) in the center, and put our meals, clothing, and other essentials closest to us in the back for quick and easy access. On a mushing trip with his girlfriend the previous winter, a moose had tried to attack Dave's dogs. He'd had to shoot and kill it. Because of that experience, and especially because we were going into grizzly country, Dave brought a gun with him. He kept it at arm's reach, just in case. When everything was packed, we dragged the sleds to the side of the road near his cabin and attempted to get some sleep. But the dogs wouldn't stop howling. They sensed what was coming.

We left Fairbanks the next day. After several more hours of loading a dozen barking dogs one at a time into the transport track above the truck, and then hauling and securing our two sleds over that, we headed north up the Dalton Highway, a relatively narrow road that extends all the way to the hulking oil-drilling rigs at Prudhoe Bay on the edge of the Arctic Ocean. Our destination was the Brooks Range, a majestic wedge of mountains that cuts across the northern half of the state. In about three or four hours we reached the Yukon River and stopped for coffee at a small truck stop run by an elderly Christian fundamentalist couple. The only traffic we saw was an occasional tractor-trailer on its way to or returning from Prudhoe Bay. The air was much colder than it had been in Fairbanks, so we both put on additional layers of clothing and checked on the dogs, who looked out at us from their wooden cubicles (which they had begun to gnaw apart). As we drove on into the night, ice fog began to set in, frosting the tundra and imparting a ghostly hue to the landscape. Near midnight, over ten hours since we had left Fairbanks, we pulled into another truck stop at the "town" of Coldfoot. The place was a genuine frontier outpost: miners, trappers, and other assorted adventurers mingling over burgers and beer. Dave and I ate dinner, bought a new headlight for our vehicle, and got directions to Nolan, an active gold-mining camp about thirty miles north of Coldfoot and the site of our starting point.

We entered the camp an hour later. Judging by my map, we were more than a hundred miles above the Arctic Circle. The dogs, deafening when we first loaded them into the truck back in Fairbanks, were still and silent by the time we reached Nolan. It was around two in the morning when we found a few of the miners still awake in one of their trailers. We had parked our truck just outside of the compound, and our hands were raw from feeding and tethering our teams barehanded in the bitter cold. The miners invited us in for coffee and to warm up—they had just gotten off their shift. We talked to them about underground gold mining, about raising dogs, about the condition of the trail we were about to mush on. Everything in Nolan was powered by generators, and a constant drone permeated the camp and our conversation.

It was numbingly cold by the time we walked back to the truck. I tried (and failed) to sleep in its enclosed cabin, while Dave slept outside underneath the transport track. My sleeping bag did little to protect me from the frigid air, which turned my breath into white smoke: the truck's windows frosted over within minutes. Our dogs slept quietly to the side of the road, each one attached by his collar to the picket line that linked them together. At dawn we got started. Before we had a chance to put food into their metal bowls, the dogs started barking. Endlessly. Only their breakfast shut them up, which gave us a few minutes of relative silence to take down our sleds, check the gear, and move our truck into a more secluded area. The trailhead was on the outskirts of the camp, a few hundred yards away from us. Our plan was to make a giant loop through a section of the Brooks Range and return to Nolan and the truck in a week.

After I gathered the bowls, Dave and I put on the dogs' harnesses and hooked them up to their respective sleds. They were fresh and excited—so excited that they lunged forward and jumped into the air in anticipation of the run. Sled dogs like it very cold, so they are at their strongest early in the morning. I learned that the hard way. When we were both safely on our sleds, we removed our anchors and raced down the road. Dave led the way to the trailhead and called for his lead dogs to turn right into the park. My team followed. We careened off the road, barreled ahead another couple of hundred yards over taiga, then entered a wooded area. As the dogs dragged me helplessly around a spruce, my sled began to tilt precariously onto one runner. Suddenly it flipped over, and I skidded face first into a pile of snow. Luckily I had held on to the sled with one hand, and the weight of my body forced the team to come to a stop (if I hadn't, they most likely would have sprinted on without me for miles). The dogs turned back and stared at me with expressions of befuddlement.

We were mushing in Gates of the Arctic National Park, and the Brooks Range was just one region within it. Dave had selected one of the more remote and spectacular chunks of interior Alaska for our trip, but after thirty minutes of mushing we ran into a major challenge. Because we had decided to make this trip in early spring, we knew that we risked encountering overflow, even in the colder areas north of the Arctic Circle. Overflow occurs when, due to rising temperatures, the upper layers of ice melt over their frozen foundation, leaving up to several feet of slush hidden beneath a paper-thin, icy veneer. What looks like a frozen river can quickly crack under the weight of a sled, ruining supplies and sometimes drowning dogs.

Wiseman Creek, which we needed to cross at several points during the first few days of our trip, was filled with overflow. It was not very deep, but because no other mushers had used our route in several weeks, we had no idea about the present condition of the creeks and rivers ahead. That left us with two alternatives. Either scrap the entire trip and return to Fairbanks or push on with the clear understanding that we were taking our chances, that when we tried to make our way back to the truck the following week we might be stranded. Dave was ambivalent. He wanted to mush, but he was worried that we could run into trouble or that I could be trapped and miss my flight back to New York. He left the decision to me. I thought about why I was there, about my self-imposed mission. And when I reflected on just what was at stake for me, the decision was easy. We moved on.

Overflow turned out to be a constant annoyance but never bad enough to force us to turn around. In the early mornings the upper layers of ice were sufficiently hard to support our sleds, but by noon they developed the consistency of a Slurpee. The two of us had to run (or often, like our teams, slip and slide) along the side of our sleds; our weight, coupled with the drag caused by the overflow, would have made the sleds too heavy for the dogs to pull. It was grueling work, and we had to repeat it whenever we had to travel over hills. At the end of each day my arms had new bruises from breaking so many falls, and my boots were usually soaked with water. The routine was the same whenever we made camp. Remove the harnesses and connect the dogs to the picket line, away from the wind (though they are comfortable in temperatures well below zero, a bitter wind can kill them). Look for dead wood to saw into small pieces for cooking and heating. Melt snow for drinking water. Feed the teams. Set up the tent. Eat dinner, drink some rum, try to go to sleep. The mornings were miserable, with temperatures five or ten degrees below zero, even at the beginning of April. Any piece of clothing that so much as brushed against water the day before was frozen stiff when we woke up. My bare fingers were so numb (our heavy mittens were too awkward and cumbersome for the task) that hooking our dogs back onto their tug lines took ten times as long as it did later in the afternoon. But after the teams were taken care of and we'd had our hot coffee, the rush of air that refreshed my face as our sleds raced out of camp made the morning's travails a distant memory.

The strenuousness of our trip made reflection difficult, but there were moments when I was mushing through a valley or over a small inland lake that I was able to absorb the beauty and achieve an almost meditative state. My worries about the Jewish world washed away. My anxiety about feeling out of place as a rabbi didn't seem to matter. I was a child of God in God's backyard, and everything was going to be all right. Taking care of my dogs was like taking care of six screaming babies, but I loved them. Even though their ceaseless barking and fighting with one another often drove me to the point of madness, I trusted my team. They were my lifeline, my link to the outside world, and I owed them my gratitude and respect. I also owed Dave. Despite all my adventures, my encounters with jail cells, grizzly bears, and mountaintops, deep down I was just another Jewish intellectual, and I knew it. Once again I was dependent on others for my well-being. I could not have made the trip without the guidance and experience of my friend. And neither of us could have made it without our canine companions.

Several days into our trip, on a Friday night, I tried to observe a makeshift Sabbath beneath the Endicott Mountains. Judaism in the rough. I took out two candles that I had packed back in New York and stuck them into the snow. Since it was spring, the midnight sun had just begun to emerge, and our campsite was draped with long shadows. I lit the candles. After I said the appropriate blessings, Dave and I ate dinner and talked in the tent about wild country and wild women until it grew dark outside. Cody, my wheel dog and Dave's pet, was with us, lying between our two sleeping bags. Dave was ready to go to bed. I told him that I wanted to go for a walk down to the river but that he should go ahead and put out the fire. The dogs, silent but watching my every step, were curled into balls to insulate themselves from the cold. I was cold, too. And tired. I had been so busy dealing with the day-to-day chores of handling my team that I had forgotten what it was that had brought me to this spot on the earth. But as I stood there alone on the ice and looked over the peaks into the purple sky, I remembered.

The dark night erupted before me. Waves of white-green light scrolled across the heavens. It was the aurora borealis, the northern lights. I had seen them before, years ago, but never from this perspective. They seemed to be directly in front of me, hovering over the mountains. Almost beckoning. Pythagoras, the early Greek philosopher, claimed that the cosmos itself could speak, that the motion of the celestial bodies was so great that they had to produce a noise. He called that sound the music of the spheres and argued that the reason humans could not hear it was that it had been with us from the moment of birth and we could not distinguish it from its opposite, silence. Yet I swear I heard something that night. Not with my ears, but with some other part of myself. I watched the pulsations of light the way you watch panthers in the wild, with awe and amazement. I knew then and there that I was in the presence of something untamed and untamable. Transcendent and mysterious. Something that warmed my blood and made my soul tremble with new life.

I'd found what I had come for. Alaska was my Sinai.

One of the problems with religion today is that our faiths, as well as our clergy, are too protective of us. They try to tame the transcendent. They shackle it with too many forces. Denominationalism. Politics. Intellectualization. Our religions often lack the divine fire that gave birth to them in the first place. And because they have failed to provide us with the sustenance that so many of us now so desperately crave, we have been forced to look elsewhere. It was this hunger, this quest for the sacred, that drove me to the wilds of Alaska and that now makes me feel at times like a vagabond in search of a home. But I am not alone. The wilderness has always exerted a pull over those who have struggled to find God in a house of worship and who sometimes had to look to the frontier for their spirituality.

A wonderful example of this impulse in the Christian world is found in the life and works of the brilliant Protestant thinker Jonathan Edwards (1703–1758). Edwards, a third-generation American, was born into a family of New England ministers. He was raised in East Windsor, Connecticut, a small frontier village. As a young boy Edwards often found solace and intellectual stimulation from nature—in the fields near his childhood home and in the river that led to the world beyond it. At thirteen he attended Yale College, then only two years old, and after he completed his education and an internship at a Scotch Presbyterian congregation in New York City, Edwards became the associate pastor in the parish of his grandfather in Northampton, Massachusetts, in 1727 and served there over the next two decades. His dramatic pulpit presence and forceful preaching inspired a revival movement in his church that soon aroused widespread interest, helping to ignite the Great Awakening that swept colonial America in the mid–eighteenth century.

Despite his prominence, Edwards lived a great part of his life in the frontier communities of New England. Much of his writing reflects his interest in and familiarity with nature and in the role that the natural world played in his religious thinking. Although he served a congregation for twenty-three years, Edwards frequently returns to the images of rivers and woods when he writes about matters of the spirit. In his "Personal Narrative," an essay he wrote in his mid-thirties about his own spiritual journey, Edwards writes that when he was a boy he "had particular secret places of my own in the woods, where I used to retire by myself; and was from time to time much affected" by his ruminations on religion and the life of the soul. He calls this period one of his "seasons of awakening." He prayed five times a day in seclusion, away from his home and church. While his early connection to nature helped to instill a rich spiritual life in the young Edwards, he lost that connection later in his teens, when he was plagued by various internal struggles and drawn to sin "like a dog to his vomit." Yet it was nature that pulled him back from the brink. His meditation on a verse from the Song of Songs, "I am a rose of Sharon, a lily of the valleys" (2:1), which to Edwards represented the beauty not only of the natural world but of God, led to intense visions "of being alone in the mountains, or some solitary wilderness, far from all mankind, sweetly conversing with Christ, and wrapt and swallowed up in God."

Nature was inextricably linked to the minister's inner life. Year after year, whenever he wanted (or needed) to find inspiration for his soul, Edwards would take long walks alone in the woods and in other solitary places "for meditation, soliloquy, and prayer," and to "converse with God." During the time he worked in New York, Edwards would often roam the banks of the Hudson River, away from the bustle and distractions of the city. One day Edwards was out walking in a secluded part of his father's pasture in East Windsor. As he looked up at the sky and clouds, he experienced a spiritual epiphany that filled him with amazement and awe: "The appearance of every thing was altered; there seemed to be, as it were, a calm, sweet, cast, or appearance of divine glory, in almost every thing. God's excellency, his wisdom, his purity and love, seemed to appear in every thing; in the sun, moon and stars; in the clouds and blue sky; in the grass, flowers, trees; in the water and all nature."

His whole way of viewing the world had changed. While earlier in life "nothing had been so terrible to me" as thunder and lightning, now these natural phenomena had become reflections of God's majesty and grace: "Before, I used to be uncommonly terrified with thunder, and to be struck with terror when I saw a thunder-storm rising; but now, on the contrary, it rejoiced me. I felt God, if I may so speak, at the first appearance of a thunder storm; and used to take the opportunity, at such times, to fix myself in order to view the clouds, and see the lightnings play, and hear the majestic and awful voice of God's thunder, which oftentimes was exceedingly entertaining, leading me to sweet contemplations of my great and glorious God." For Edwards, the phenomena and activities of nature were merely masks for the presence of God, images and representations of the divine will. Unmasked in this way, even nature's most riveting displays no longer instilled him with fear. But the seeds of this new worldview were buried in his childhood. When he was a boy, after having seen a rainbow in the sky, Edwards sketched a picture of one and then wrote down some questions about it as well as possible answers. He ended the piece with the following words: "The next Grand Question is what is it Causes the Colours of the Rainbow?" From an early age Edwards knew that questions necessarily lead to other questions, that the concrete, in the mind of a thoughtful person, always leads to the abstract.

Later in his life Edwards created a homemade notebook, *The Images of Divine Things, The Shadows of Divine Things, The Language and Lessons of Nature.* The manuscript contains 212 entries, each of which is presumed to be the earthly image of a spiritual truth. It concludes with an essay called "The Beauty of the World." Although Edwards had not intended to publish the work in its disjointed and somewhat fragmentary form, it nonetheless possesses a thematic integrity that transcends its structural problems. As he observed the physical world of trees and streams, moon and stars, birds and beasts, Edwards saw each part as a "shadow" of metaphysical reality. The person with a pure soul and an acute mind could read these signs and types as the language of God.

Edwards argues that the "immense magnificence of the visible world in inconceivable vastness, the incomprehensible height of the heavens, etc., is but a type of the infinite magnificence, height and glory of God's work in the spiritual world: the most incomprehensible expression of His power, wisdom, holiness and love in what is wrought and brought to pass in the world." The terrestrial world mirrors, or serves as a *representation* of, the celestial one. The depths of the oceans, the enormity of the firmament, and the beauty of earth's creatures are the images and shadows of those same qualities that God possesses to an infinite degree. For Edwards, the spiritual mysteries are "signified and typified in the constitution of the natural world." To a trained eye and reflective mind, the growth of a spruce is not just the product of natural laws, but a sign of divine providence. And the aurora borealis is not only a swath of light particles reacting to a magnetic field. It is the breath of God.

In "The Beauty of the World," Edwards discusses the idea of resemblance. For him, "the sweetest and most charming beauty" of the natural world is "its resemblance of spiritual beauties." The world is a harmony, an ordered and interdependent composite of living creatures and natural forces. The "decent trust, dependence and acknowledgment in the planets continually moving around the sun, receiving his influences by which they are made happy, bright and beautiful" resembles the way the world and its inhabitants relate to their Creator. The interplay and balance of sounds, colors, smells, and motions are a resemblance "of every grace and beautiful disposition of mind, of an inferiour towards a superiour cause, preserver, benevolent benefactor, and a fountain of happiness." Soaring birds seem to embody freedom and joy. Flowers seem to express a panoply of passions. Our world is a mirror image of the divine world. None of the features of nature—neither the music of the spheres nor the rhythm of the waves—are merely what they appear to be. If we observe them closely, we can remove their veils and transform them into the language of a transcendental reality.

Through his writings on nature, Edwards makes it clear that for him religion is not about creed or ritual, but about inner experience. The fact that Edwards had first lived out what he later wrote about helped to win him the respect and admiration of his Northampton congregation and the wider Christian community. But relations between pulpit and pew soured. In 1750, because of a conflict within his parish over financial and other matters, Edwards was dismissed from his pastorate after twenty-three years of service. In a state of virtual exile from his former life, he spent the next six years as a missionary to the Housatonic Indians at a rugged frontier outpost in Stockbridge, Massachusetts, during which time he wrote some of his best-known works. In 1757 he became the president of the College of New Jersey (now Princeton), but he died there in an epidemic the following year.

At about the same period on the other side of the Atlantic, a new religious movement was also emerging in the Jewish world. By the beginning of the eighteenth century the once robust Jewish communities of Poland were in tatters. Over the previous decade a rebellion by Ukrainian peasants against their Polish overlords and a war with Sweden had taken their toll on Jews, who were often used as scapegoats or otherwise caught up in the brutality and violence. As a result, Polish Jewry recoiled from the outside world and turned inward, constructing a Judaism that was severe, prohibitive, ritualistic, and highly cerebral. The only activity that offered relief from the toil of daily life was the learning of Torah—but that was open solely to the elite. The poverty, suffering, and sense of being stifled (or even trapped) that defined the Jewish world at that time led to an ever-intensifying desire among the masses for revolution.

It was in this atmosphere of social turbulence and spiritual crisis that Israel ben Eliezer of Miedzyboz (1700–1760), known by all as the Baal Shem Tov, came onto the scene. Though he never wrote a book, and all we know about his life and teachings has been handed down to us through obviously embellished and exaggerated legends, the Baal Shem Tov founded a new, radical religious movement—Hasidism—and influenced thousands of Jews in his own era and beyond. He was a teacher and a healer, a leader and a charismatic who was able to reach a population that was unmoved by the rarefied rabbinic elite. For the Baal Shem, scholarly learning is not the only way to God. One can approach the divine through other means, such as the emotions (joy, hope, love, prayer) or the experiences of the everyday world (food, drink, music, a sunrise). Natural phenomena and physical activities are the manifestations of the divine. It is in *this* world, not on some heavenly plateau, that we must seek God.

Nature, and our relationship to it, is central to the Baal Shem's worldview. What makes this fact so fascinating is that, unlike the visions of the Buddha or St. Francis of Assisi, the Baal Shem's spiritual vision was formed not in the shade of pleasant groves or on green hills dotted with olive trees, but in narrow streets, small, musty rooms, and dirty public squares. His was a mysticism of the shtetl, a spirituality for the marketplace. Perhaps his interest in nature was related to the collective yearning of his people for something beautiful, something that would transcend their impoverished condition. For that reason, many of the stories about the Baal Shem that involve the natural world have a strong mythic quality to them. As the Jewish thinker Martin Buber notes, myth is the expression of the fullness of existence, its image and its sign. In the telling of stories and parables, the link between spirit and nature is revealed, the features of nature serving as symbols of divine truths—or even of divinity itself. In the Hasidism of the Baal Shem, mysticism and mythic saga merge into a single stream.

In one story, "The Language of the Birds," Rabbi Arye, a preacher from Polonnoye, seeks out the wisdom of the Baal Shem Tov. He had heard that the Baal Shem could understand the language of all creatures, that he could grasp what the animals on the earth and in the sky shared with one another about the secrets of their existence. The Baal Shem could discern the conversations of trees and plants, and when he laid his ear to the soil or to rock, he could hear the whispers of the creatures who dwell below, in crevices and caves. After a long journey, Rabbi Arye finally reaches the hasidic master. At first the Baal Shem ignores him. But after several tests and additional journeys, the Baal Shem invites the rabbi to accompany him to a place in the countryside, in the cornfields outside of town.

"Sit nearer to me and bend your ear to my mouth," the Baal Shem tells him, "for I shall now teach you my wisdom." He then proceeds to explain how it is only the person with a pure heart and an elevated soul who can apprehend the mysteries of the universe and the meaning of all the sounds of the earth. That individual "hears the voices under the earth conversing in the nights when to the human race the silence seems complete and every sound appears to have died away. The voices of the animals on the earth and the birds in the air convey to him those secrets which the senses of man ordinarily cannot perceive. Thus for him the world is never silent. It presses forward to him with every wonder; nothing is unyielding and nothing denies itself to him." For the Baal Shem, the sounds of earth's creatures (like the beauties of nature were for Jonathan Edwards) are, to the initiated, merely the images or shadows of a higher cosmic reality. They are the language of illumination. When the Baal Shem had finished speaking, he led Rabbi Arye into a forest, and the rabbi's ears suddenly filled with the song of creation.

In another story, a Hasid who was traveling to Miedzyboz to spend the Day of Atonement near the Baal Shem was forced to take an unexpected pause in his journey. That evening, when the stars began to rise (and he could no longer travel because it was now Kol Nidre), he was still far from the town and had no choice but to pray alone in an open field. When he finally arrived in Miedzyboz after the holy day was over, the Baal Shem received him with a joyfulness and cordiality that seemed especially enthusiastic. "Your praying," he told the Hasid, "lifted up all the prayers which were lying stored in that field." Edwards writes that the natural world shares a resemblance with the spiritual world. Through this legend, the Baal Shem conveys a similar message: Nature itself can praise God, and also serve as a place for spirituality as profound and appropriate as any house of worship. In this case, it is the partnership between a human being and a remote field that creates a religious experience worthy of the holiest day of the Jewish year.

For me, it was the Brooks Range that inspired me to continue my journey as a rabbi during a period of doubt and despair. Though certain features of nature (such as mountains) do not seem to possess what we would call "souls," at times they nonetheless have ways of protecting us from falling into the pit. One colorful parable about the Baal Shem shows him hiking as a young man over the mountains near his home. When he wanted to meditate, he would climb to the peaks and remain there for a time. Once he was so deep in mystical rapture that he failed to notice how close he was to the edge of an abyss. As he got up from his meditation and started to walk on, unaware that he was about to step into dead air, a neighboring mountain leaped immediately to the spot, pressed itself against the other mountain, and allowed the Baal Shem to continue safely on his journey. While this tale is surely more myth than historical reality, it illustrates the redemptive role that nature can play in our spiritual lives. Not only can nature's beauty elevate us when we are experiencing inner despondency; its humbling majesty can also guard us from another kind of darkness, that of succumbing to the dangers of self-absorption.

The Baal Shem did not hear the divine call until well into his thirties, and the site where he heard it was a grotto in the Carpathian Mountains. One morning, as Israel ben Eliezer was contemplating alone in the cavern as he had done many times before, the walls suddenly seemed to whisper to him. Voices spoke to him. From the arch at the entrance there thundered a mysterious command. This went on for several days, the command growing louder, more urgent, and more irresistible to the Baal Shem. He heard the hour of his revelation approaching. Then there came a morning when everything around him became clear, when he understood all, when the secrets of divine knowledge entered into his soul. The command grew silent.

And, like Nietzsche's Zarathustra, the Baal Shem Tov made his descent from the mountains, ready at last to reveal himself to the world.

Clearly, nature can serve as a context or even a catalyst for deep spiritual encounter. That experience can be as dramatic and cacophonous as the theophany at Mount Sinai or as subtle and muted as the "still small voice" that Elijah hears in the wilderness of the desert. But an interesting element that many of these encounters share is sound. The Baal Shem comments on the hidden language of animals and fields. Jonathan Edwards describes the singing of birds and the roaring of rivers as the individual notes of a great symphony. These are not new ideas. Pythagoras may have been one of the earliest thinkers to write about the existence of celestial music, but years later Plutarch explains our difficulty in hearing it in purely *spiritual* terms. For him, humanity cannot normally hear this cosmic song because our souls are imprisoned, stopped up "not with wax but with carnal obstructions and passions." Nature can open our souls and unblock our ears. The Hebrew word for world is *olam,* which, in the Kabbalah, has the same numerical value as the word for concealment, and the word for nature is *teva,* which has the same value as the word for God. Thus, while the everyday world can hide God from us, it is in (and sometimes through) nature that the reality of transcendence and the voice of heaven are revealed to us.

Still, no one should have to travel to the Arctic or to journey through the desert in order to find spiritual fulfillment. It is the message, not the channel through which it is conveyed, that is of primary import. Religion can transmit that message. But religion will have transformative power only if it allows for moments of transcendence. And transcendence is not something we can easily measure, control, or put on an altar. It is as wild as a grizzly. As ungraspable as the northern lights. Flashes of transcendence are the sparks of divinity, very real, very present, but, like a flickering flame, ultimately intangible and indefinable. That is the point where we experience God: in the cloud of unknowing, at the edge. Though we are usually able to experience only the traces of that unknowable mystery, just the brush against them, if they are left unfettered by human hands, can change our lives forever.

8 / views from the bridge

The Messiah will come only when he is no longer necessary; he will come only on the day after his arrival; he will come, not on the last day, but on the very last.

FRANZ KAFKA, "The Coming of the Messiah"

Three years ago on Passover, a novelist friend of mine invited me to join him at his annual seder. One of the guests at his table, a writer herself, ran something called the "Religion Community" on the Microsoft Network. In between the blessings over matzah and wine and our discussions about the Exodus and redemption, she told me about the community and the new possibilities for religious life on the Internet. At the end of the millennium and the edge of technology, "virtual" religious communities were beginning to form; a new generation of seekers was starting to tap into a world of information and ideas that was unknown only years before. The Internet was hot. Spirituality was in. Why not take faith on-line? At the end of our meal she told me she needed a new rabbi for the Judaism Community and asked if I was interested. The opportunity to be a rabbi at this new frontier seemed too good to pass up. Despite my inexperience with the Internet and my fears about feeling like a technological Neanderthal, I accepted.

I am now the rabbi of a *cyber*synagogue. In many ways what I do on the Internet is starkly different from the work I do as a pulpit rabbi. For one thing, this congregation is open twenty-four hours a day. Those who have pressing concerns or questions can leave them on "Ask the Rabbi" and they'll get a response from me long before most of my colleagues would even receive the message. While you can't perform a bris or conduct a funeral over the Internet, for many people that lack of focus on ritual is itself an enticement. Those turned off by organized religion but open to spiritual issues often find themselves drawn to our section of cyberspace. And because there is no control over who joins our community, not all of our members are Jews. As Abraham welcomed the three strangers into his tent, I welcome our visitors (even the occasional evangelist who tries to convert me) as honored guests. We are as ecumenical as a religious entity can be.

In other ways my work is surprisingly similar to that of a conventional cleric. My "lectern" may be made of wires instead of wood, but I still use it to preach my sermons, give religious instruction, and offer rabbinic opinion. I might not teach adult education classes to congregants while they are seated around a table, but I talk about the Jewish tradition with Internet users every day (and intermittently conduct live discussions on various topics in our Judaism chat room). I may not have an actual office for private counseling or confidential conversation, but I do have an e-mail address for those situations where discretion or personal, one-on-one communication is required. I have led some people through the mourning process and helped others trace their religious genealogies. And though I did not do the matchmaking at a congregational picnic, three of our married assistants met their spouses on-line.

Many of the especially interesting exchanges usually take place on "Ask the Rabbi." Sometimes I try to generate discussion on it by asking questions or making comments of my own, to which my "congregants" then respond. When I first started serving the Judaism Community—only one of many faith communities on the Internet, including Christianity, Islam, Buddhism, even paganism—I asked the subscribers what kind of a rabbi they were looking for:

> I'd like to ask a question of all of you. What is it that YOU want in a rabbi? A traditional model of a rabbi as teacher? A communal model of a rabbi as judge or arbiter? A mystical model of a rabbi as healer and spiritual guide? A contemporary model of a rabbi as religious "M.C."/presider over life cycle and other events? Your answers will be very useful to me, and to all of us in the post-modern Jewish world trying to find new ways of attracting Jews to their Judaism. . . .

Asking a question like this in a conventional congregation would have been difficult, if not impossible. So many factors go into the relationship between spiritual leaders and their congregations—managerial, financial, and psychological, to name just a few—that even minor issues can get horrendously complicated. Touching a subject as large as the role of a rabbi in a particular religious community is a recipe for conflict.

At one of my former "real" synagogues, when a particularly wealthy member thought his opinion was not carrying the weight it deserved, he threatened to leave the temple. Another member who hated public speaking refused, despite my urging, to make known her view on a controversial issue at an important meeting. But in a *virtual* congregation, where distinctions among congregants do not exist and where boundaries between clergy and laity are more relaxed and less intimidating, I received a great deal of feedback and have been able to adjust my rabbinate accordingly. With no building to maintain or budget to balance, our cybersynagogue allows democracy to flourish. No congregant can withdraw his support for the capital campaign. No clique can monopolize power. No rabbi can dictate policy.

Like many Americans, most of the users I encounter in the newsgroup have problems with religious practice. They are often non-observant and find little meaning in ancient rituals or indecipherable liturgies. But just the fact that they are in the newsgroup—and meeting me at the very edge of a new form of religious expression—is significant. They, like many of the rest of us in American society, are yearning for something more, something that will enrich their lives and root them in a spiritual community. Historically, religion has been defined by boundaries and parameters, distinctions in beliefs, holy books, practices, calendars. The Internet has no boundaries. I once asked our users about the notion of creating *new* rituals, ones that speak more to our own experiences:

> I'd like to know what you think of the idea of new rituals, new mitzvot [ritual behaviors]. In the Bible, there is no mention of saying the kiddush [blessing] over wine on the Sabbath—that was a rabbinic tradition created hundreds of years later after the Temple was destroyed and animal sacrifice was no longer possible as a principal mode of religious expression. Why can't we create new blessings/rites that speak to today's social/existential situation? What about a blessing to recite upon giving birth? For experiencing menopause? A new ritual to mark a child's going off to college? Are there (or should there be) any boundaries?

The responses I received to this posting were overwhelmingly positive. Most of those who wrote back had never before even considered the idea of creating new religious rituals and rites. They had always viewed Judaism as a monolithic tradition with a set, fixed system of behaviors and beliefs. Many were simply thankful that a rabbi had asked their opinion on a matter of such religious significance. One woman described how powerful a moment it was for her family when their first child went off to college and how she wished she'd had some kind of ceremony to punctuate the occasion. She proposed some new ways to mark this life cycle event and was sent additional suggestions and advice from others in the newsgroup. I was witnessing and participating in a faith community at work, caring about one another's spiritual needs, offering words of support and encouragement. While not all of the ideas that are generated online are equally good (one teenager argued for a new blessing to be recited at the time of a boy's first wet dream), I am strongly attracted to the free, uncensored exchange of views, an exchange that would be extremely difficult outside the Internet.

Usually I am not the one who asks the questions. Most of the time I respond to the queries of others. "Ask the Rabbi," like everything on the Internet, is open to anyone, regardless of a person's particular faith. Often I get questions about Jewish theology and practice from Christians or Muslims, and I strive to answer with sensitivity and thoughtfulness. The majority of the postings, though, are from Jews who want to know more about their heritage. Some of the questions they ask me are very specific. One man asked me to tell him more about the prophet Elijah. I answered him as succinctly as I could:

> Elijah is viewed historically as the harbinger of the messianic age, the "announcer" of the Messiah. That is why, as an embodied symbol of future redemption, Elijah appears at the Passover seder (Elijah's cup), at the bris [circumcision] ceremony (Elijah's chair), and at other key Jewish events and moments. Elijah is viewed almost mystically as a kind of guardian angel as well, a spiritual force who is forever on watch over the Jewish people.

Some of the questions I am asked are much more general and harder to answer in as straightforward a manner. In response to a question about how to make Judaism more attractive to this generation of Jews, I wrote:

> The answer is surely not through the construction of more Holocaust museums. But we can't look to the synagogue or the rabbis for the answers. Our tradition has always been a populist one—it has been created and re-created according to our people's needs at particular times. The place where that love of Judaism will most likely take root today isn't at religious school but in our own homes. If we want our kids to love Judaism, then we must love it ourselves. And if our rabbis are offering services that are dry and stuffy, then we must DEMAND an alternative that is inspiring, informal, and warm. In a post-Holocaust, post-Israel world, our situation requires a paradigm shift, perhaps one as radical as the shift from biblical Judaism (sacrifices, Temple, priests) to rabbinic Judaism (liturgies, synagogues, rabbis). What exactly Judaism in the twenty-first century ought to look like is unclear. What it CAN'T look like, however, is becoming clearer every day.

There are great benefits to being the rabbi of a cybersynagogue. Yet this new medium poses new problems. On the Internet, a single individual can cause great damage. With few control mechanisms, anybody can say almost anything to anyone. One of our Jewish participants has been so intolerant, disrespectful, and offensive toward those of other faiths—as well as toward fellow Jews—that I have tried to have him banned from the newsgroup. I have not succeeded. Potential legal and public relations issues have prevented any action, and he has continued to insult and alienate our members as well as interfere with my ability to do my job properly. My cyberclergy colleagues face similar problems with troublemakers in their own newsgroups. Flesh-and-blood members of a real congregation would not put up with this situation. Free speech is and should be a cherished American value, but when it is abused (as it sometimes is on the Internet) it can be profoundly destructive to the well-being of a community.

At a time when religion has been deconstructed and decentralized, few media reach as many potential "congregants" as the Internet. We never have to look for extra chairs to accommodate overflow crowds. Millions of believers can join us from anywhere in the world. The anonymity that a virtual religious community confers encourages people to speak more candidly. But in the absence of face-to-face encounters, relationships among members of our community will always be limited. Nothing will ever be able to replace the embrace of another human being or the feeling of families at prayer. Contact is not communication. We may all be created in the image of God, but only the shadows of those images will be visible on-line. The Internet is not a godsend, but a mixed blessing. It draws people together at the same time that it distances them. It expands the horizons of religion while collapsing its moorings and traditions. Contemporary faith stands at the cutting edge of technology. It may have also reached its final frontier.

Mainstream religion is in trouble and in transition. Many Americans, especially younger ones, are turning away from the churches and synagogues of their parents and grandparents. In the new millennium they find little meaning in ancient liturgies and little power in unfamiliar rituals. Services often seem formal and cold. Sermons put them to sleep. Sometimes the whole institution of organized religion, with its outwardly arcane array of practices, observances, and beliefs, seems like something from another planet. But in postmodern America, in a culture of unprecedented freedom and multiple options, God is no longer consigned to our classical houses of worship. Most people today feel little discomfort about exploring their spiritual identities outside of traditional venues and, in a growing number of cases, even outside of traditional faiths.

In addition to religious life on the Internet, other new forms of spiritual expression are beginning to emerge. Most cities have meditation schools. Religious retreat centers and summer camps, which create powerful and transformative immersion experiences, are springing up all over the country. Muslims study the Koran in corporate boardrooms, and Jews and Christians discuss the Bible over breakfast. Some congregations have developed "prayer centers," where worship services of different types and with diverse—and at times divergent—theological viewpoints (environmentalist, egalitarian, feminist, traditional) take place simultaneously and under one roof. I have been the rabbi-in-residence for Jewish adventure travel trips, programs that combine the excitement of rugged outdoor challenges like rock climbing and whitewater rafting with informal but intensive religious education.

Yet none of this is new. While these particular forms of religious life are fresh and innovative, the dynamic behind them is ancient. Change has been a constant throughout the history of religion and spirituality. New situations have called for new approaches; politics, economics, conquest, culture, and even climate have all been factors in the creation and unfolding of different traditions. Canons are not born; they are made. The scriptures that are held sacred by both Jews and Christians began as a set of just five books, the Torah, and only later—after centuries of historical developments—expanded to include books of judges, kings, prophets, proverbs, and psalms. As more time passed, Christianity added still more books to its canon and constructed a second, "new" testament. Religions, like their holy books, are made up of layers—they grow with the ages. But not forever. Sometimes circumstances force a (wanted or unwanted) transition, a (partial or, in periods of crisis, total) break with the past and a shift toward the future. And when the old forms of religious life are removed or made obsolete, new ones must fill the void. Without this bridge, this leap from one ledge to another, religion itself would die out.

In the biblical books of Ezra and Nehemiah, we see an early instance of one of these bridges at work in the Israelite community. In the year 586 B.C.E., under the command of King Nebuchadnezzer, the Babylonian army smashed a rebellion in the land of Judah (which it had conquered and occupied two decades earlier), slaughtered thousands, ransacked Jerusalem, and burned the sacred Temple in its heart. Large numbers of the people of Israel were forced to live in exile, deported to Babylonia under pain of death. Their entire spiritual way of life had been wiped out. With no more Temple or holy vessels, the priesthood effectively became irrelevant; animal sacrifice, the community's primary mode of serving God in Judah, was rendered pointless; Jerusalem, the country's capital and the site of religious pilgrimages, was destroyed, out of Israelite hands, and many hundreds of miles away.

Whatever problems the Jewish community or my rabbinic colleagues and I are facing today pale in comparison with the tribulations and uncertainties of this harrowing period. The rants of a few neo-Nazis in Idaho are far less threatening to Jewish survival than were the conditions of 2,500 years ago. In Psalm 137 we get a taste of some of the sentiments and sorrows that the Jewish Diaspora community experienced in Babylonia: "By the waters of Babylon, there we sat down and wept, when we remembered Zion." Their prior religious culture had been demolished, and while many Jews tried to make the best of the exile experience, lamentation seemed to be the predominant expression of the community's collective mood ("How shall we sing the Lord's song in a foreign land?").

But in 539 B.C.E., Cyrus the Great conquered Babylonia and

established Persia as the major imperial power of the ancient Near East. In contrast with their predecessors, the Persians presented themselves to their vassal-states as a benevolent force. Displaced and exiled peoples within the empire (including the Jews) were encouraged to return to their ancestral homelands and to reestablish their local political and religious institutions. The exiled Jewish community in Babylonia viewed Cyrus as a liberator and saw his work as part of a divine plan for national redemption; the Bible puts the following words into the mouth of the king: "All the kingdoms of the earth has the Lord, the God of heaven, given me; and He has charged me to build Him a house in Jerusalem, which is in Judah. Whosoever there is among you of all His people—his God be with him—let him go up to Jerusalem, which is in Judah, and build the house of the Lord, the God of Israel, He is the God who is in Jerusalem." (Ezra 1:2–3)

We can imagine the excitement that must have rippled through the Babylonian Jewish community. Whenever people return from a long separation from someone or something we miss and love, we often desire (and secretly hope) that things will be as they were when we left them. The Jews were no different and immediately set out to try to reconstruct the religion that they remembered. Their repatriation to the land of Judah occurred in successive waves, the first taking place not long after the Persian conquest and led by Sheshbazzar, who brought back the Temple's holy vessels and laid the foundation for the rebuilt structure. He was followed by Zerubbabel, who, with the high priest Joshua, established an altar on the Temple Mount and completed rebuilding the Second Temple in 516 B.C.E.

Yet things were not exactly the same. Though the outer appearances of religious life in Palestine were restored to the way they had looked before the exile, new factors, both internal and external, were beginning to fashion a new kind of Jewish spiritual practice. Many years had passed since the initial deportations, and most of the reconstruction of the Jewish state was performed by leaders who came from—and were influenced by the culture and traditions of—Babylonia. In the books of Ezra and Nehemiah, the local population (who had remained in Judah) is looked down on, and the only Jews allowed to serve as Temple personnel or in leadership positions were the ones from the Diaspora communities. The Samaritans to the north offered to help Zerubbabel when he started to rebuild the Temple, arguing that they too were worshippers of the God of Israel. But at a time in which new boundaries and definitions needed to be set, he rejected their assistance, and the Samaritans eventually built their own temple on Mount Gerizim.

In 458 B.C.E. a fresh wave of exiles, led by Ezra, returned to Judah. Ezra himself embodied a new type of religious leader. He was not a prophet or priest, but "a scribe skilled in the law of Moses." (Ezra 7:6) The figure of the scribe, a kind of "protorabbi," represented a new office in the Jewish religious community, one that concerned itself with the promulgation and interpretation of sacred text. Ezra is sometimes referred to as "the father of Judaism" because he initiated a new religious system based on the knowledge and observance of the Torah, the Jewish constitution. While the Temple cult remained active during this period, a transition was already taking place, a bridge that began to lead away from cultic practice toward public reading and worship. And in an age (like our own) of spiritual restructuring, it is understandable why Ezra (like most of the Jewish leaders of today) was worried about the harmful effects of intermarriage with other religious groups, making its prohibition a central aspect of his teaching. That is the tension inherent in any transition: trying to balance outward expansion into new and necessary territories while at the same time protecting an inner anchor of self-identity.

The restoration of Jewish life in Judah continued with Nehemiah, who served two terms as governor of Jerusalem, starting in 445 B.C.E. Under his administrations, the gates and walls of the capital were rebuilt; Jerusalem was repopulated; economic and cultic reforms were instituted; Jewish control was established over the cultural and commercial life of the city; and Ezra's legislation regarding mixed marriages was enforced. Though the Jewish population in the country during the Persian period was much smaller than it was in pre-Exilic times (and would not return to a similar level for several hundred years), owing to the leadership and vision of Ezra and Nehemiah it was the site of dynamic internal activity and profound transformation. The Jewish state and Jewish spirituality were reconstructed on the ruins of their past—but with an eye toward their future.

There was not much time to pause and take stock. In 332 B.C.E. Alexander the Great conquered the land of Judah (which came to be known as Judea), and Hellenism was propagated, by strategic design, throughout the region. In earlier conquests Israel had remained at the edge of world empires, far from seats of power and removed from urban centers and international highways; with the Greek occupation it became a focal point—and a perpetual battlefield—among competing regional powers. With no cultural insulation and little political stability, Judea's residents, and the development of the Jewish religion, were hurled into a state of incessant flux, under constant pressure from outside forces and influences. For a brief period of time, following the successful Maccabean revolt in 166 B.C.E. (that we honor even now during the festival of Hanukkah), Judea became an independent Jewish state, the first time since the days of David and Solomon that the land was united and under Jewish rule.

But conquest came again from the West. Jewish sovereignty was lost once more, this time to the Romans when Pompey conquered Judea in 63 B.C.E. For over a century Judea was run by the likes of Herod, Pontius Pilate, and other generally loathsome puppet rulers. It was a period of turbulence and social ferment. There was conflict between the Jews and the Romans, the rich and the poor, the residents of cities and those in rural areas. There was also strife *within* the Jewish religious community—far worse than anything we see today transpiring among the various denominations, such as Reform, Conservative, or Orthodox. In the priesthood itself competition and corruption permeated the ranks of the upper and lower clergy. Pharisees and Sadducees vied for power and influence. Jewish zealots in favor of open rebellion against Roman rule collided, often violently and sometimes fatally, with a religious establishment that favored cooperation, negotiation, and legal protest. Some of the religious revolutionaries, like the Essenes, believed they were living at the end of days and fled south, deep into the desert, forming sectarian communities and waiting for Armageddon to arrive. Renegade prophets of gloom and doom roamed the countryside. A few claimed to be the Messiah.

This was the setting for yet another bridge moment in Jewish history, perhaps one of the most important and far-reaching. In the fall of 66 C.E. a group called the Sicarii ("daggermen") entered Jerusalem. In addition to doing battle with the Roman soldiers who were stationed there and whose numbers had been somewhat diminished by earlier riots in the city, these Jews also attacked the Jewish aristocracy, killing priests and nobility alike whom they accused of being Roman sympathizers. Though the Sicarii were eventually put down by a faction of priests, the revolutionary spark had already been ignited, and new bands of fighters took their place in violent confrontation with Rome. For the next four years, until the siege of Jerusalem and the destruction of the Second Temple in 70 C.E., the great Jewish revolt roiled the land.

The Jewish leaders in Jerusalem faced stark choices. As in many revolutions, those who favored accommodation or compromise were accused of being traitors. Some were killed. Many chose, out of either belief or fear, to side with the revolutionaries and fight. But there is a famous story in the Talmud about the controversial actions of one of the key figures of that time, Rabban Yohanan ben Zakkai, who chose a different path. After walking through the marketplace during the heat of the siege, he sees a group of starving men making stew out of nothing but straw (since the Romans had cut off the city from its supply lines and the zealots, in an effort to instill in Jerusalem's inhabitants the sense that they had nothing to lose by fighting, had deliberately burned the stores of wheat and barley). He asks himself: "Can men who are reduced to cooking straw and drinking its water withstand Vespasian's troops? Matters cannot be remedied unless I go out of the city." Concerned that the zealots are dangerously misguided and dragging the Jewish people—and the Jewish religion—to the edge of destruction, he devises what he considers a plan for spiritual survival.

He invites Abba Sicara, the chief of the zealots, to meet with him in secret. When Abba Sicara arrives, Rabban Yohanan admonishes him: "How long will you men continue what you are doing? You are killing all the people by famine." Abba Sicara replies, "What choice do I have? If I dare object to them, they will kill me." He goes on to explain that the zealots have made a pact among themselves not to allow anyone out of the city except as a corpse (in order to enforce "loyalty" to the revolutionary cause). But Rabban Yohanan has a response for him, a response that many think saved the Jewish people—as well as Judaism itself: "Then have me taken out as a corpse."

Rabban Yohanan pretends to fall ill and die, and his disciples construct a coffin for him. He is carried beyond the gates of the city and brought to Vespasian, who has just been appointed emperor and must now return to Rome. After Rabban Yohanan impresses him with a show of his wisdom, Vespasian says to the Jewish leader: "I am now going away from here and will send someone else to take my place [Titus]. You may, however, make a request of me, and I will grant it." Rabban Yohanan says that he wants to set up a small rabbinical academy in a tiny town: "Give me Yavneh and its sages." He does not ask for personal riches or power. What he desires is a gateway to the Jewish future.

The imagery is poignant. Faced with the death of his people and culture, Rabban Yohanan finds a bridge to renewed life, a pathway to spiritual resurrection. Even though this tale is ultimately one of success and survival, it always feels tragic to me when I read it. While it is about the passage of Judaism into the rabbinic age, it is also about the violent end of the biblical era. The Temple is destroyed for a second and final time. There has been widespread suffering, destruction, and death. The Jewish people have been scattered all over the world, producing a new Diaspora. In order for their religious life to continue, Jews had no choice but to change Judaism, to make it transportable, to imbue it with features that would allow it to flourish under any conditions. It had to be adaptable, flexible (in its fundamental structure) to new situations and unforeseen environments. In the wake of the great Jewish revolt, and after the creation of the school at Yavneh, the rabbinate supplanted the priesthood, the synagogue eclipsed the Temple, and liturgy and prayer replaced animal sacrifice. Though these institutions and offices had already been present many years, Yavneh and its scholars accelerated the process of religious transformation and revitalization, restructuring Judaism into the familiar form that we know today.

One of the greatest turning points in Christianity came at about the same time that Judaism was in the initial throes of this transformation. In the beginning of the first century Jesus was active on the Palestinian scene, traveling throughout the land and preaching his message to all those who would listen. But in 30 C.E., just days after he had entered Jerusalem, he was put to death by the Romans. His earliest disciples were Jews, and the group they formed was treated by some as simply another Jewish sect (like the Essenes who were living in the desert to the south). In Mark, often considered the most historically reliable of the gospel texts because of its primacy in age, Jesus is depicted as a normal man, the disciple of a wandering ascetic named John the Baptist (possibly an Essene himself). As I mentioned earlier, there were many holy men, faith healers, and preachers of the end of days roaming around the region at this time. Jesus was not a unique religious figure, and a number of his teachings place him comfortably within the Jewish prophetic and even Pharisaic traditions.

During his life, Jesus never claimed in clear terms to be God. After his death, however, his followers came to believe that he was, a human incarnation of divinity who walked among them and who would one day return. What had once viewed itself as a Jewish sect had gradually become a distinct Gentile faith with its own conception of God and separate set of spiritual practices (though I have argued tooth and nail with many "Jews for Jesus" in our own era who claim, profoundly misguidedly, that one can believe both in Judaism and in a divine Jesus simultaneously). No one did more to develop and spread this new religion than Paul, a Jew himself. Paul was, and continues to be, a controversial figure. For Jews he is the paradigmatic apostate; for Christians he is the model apostle.

In 35 C.E., somewhere near Damascus, Paul underwent a conversion experience and became a follower of Jesus. The vast majority of other Jews had rejected the divinity of Jesus and the resultant "Jewish Christianity" of some of their contemporaries. Paul saw his mission as different from that of his peers, who viewed their task as trying to bring in other Jews to the discipleship of Jesus. Paul believed that the Gospel should also be brought to the Gentiles, and he preached the teachings of Jesus in Syria, Asia Minor, Macedonia, and Greece. He was convinced that non-Jews could become full-fledged members of the New Israel, even if they did not observe the laws of the Torah. This approach offended the original group of disciples, who still wanted to be treated as Jews and ultimately broke with Paul over the issue. But it led to a greatly enlarged pool of potential Christians and an enormous expansion of Christianity.

Peter and James had presented the teachings of Jesus as the apex of Judaism. Paul had transformed them into the cornerstones of a new faith. Here we have a clear example of a religious bridge moment in action, or what Christian theologian Hans Küng terms a "paradigm shift." Thanks largely to the efforts of Paul, Jewish Christianity had become Hellenistic Gentile Christianity, a religion that was "liberated" from the Law of Moses, a tradition that was rooted more in "love" than in law (Christian catchphrases that most of us now view as little more than anti-Jewish sound bites). During most of the first century, Christians conceived of and prayed to God like Jews, but by the 80s they were formally expelled from the synagogues because they no longer observed the precepts of the Torah, such as circumcision, dietary rules, and Sabbath prohibitions.

Because of Paul, a Gentile could become a Christian without having to first become a Jew. The consequences of this transition are staggering, and they affected not only the inner and outer structures of Christianity, but the entire Western world. By moving, both strategically and theologically, from the center of Jewish life to its periphery, Paul began the process of Christianizing the communities of the Mediterranean and beyond; he helped to forge a new and distinct identity for Christianity, in contrast with the Jewish Christians, who in external behavior at least more closely resembled their Jewish neighbors; he was the catalyst for the transformation of a marginal spiritual movement into a world religion. In many respects Paul was the key to establishing a Hellenistic Christian culture and a concept of a "church," religious phenomena that would intensify in scope and in intensity under the reign of the Roman emperor Constantine.

By the third century Christianity had become one of the most prevalent religions in the Roman Empire. Unlike the underground "mystery cults" and small groups of desert ascetics that existed during the time of the Roman persecutions, more and more Christians were now living in urban areas and leading urbane lives. Their Hellenistic sensibilities demanded—and helped to form—a religion that was more mainstream, a force of order and stability rather than one of agitation. This appealed to the emperor Constantine, who in 312 became a Christian himself and made Christianity legal the following year. With Christianity as the official religion of the empire, it received the political imprimatur that propelled it far beyond the confines of its earlier status. What had begun as a persecuted sect pleading for toleration soon became a religious institution that demanded conformity to its own rules and creeds.

The increase in the number of adherents to Christianity that resulted from this edict led to an increase in the diversity of their theological beliefs. While today the various Christian denominations and their different belief systems are accepted as a given, 1,700 years ago the theological debates were so fundamental and had become so heated that they threatened to tear the early church apart. The central controversy revolved around a single question: Was Jesus (the redeemer of human souls) identical with God (the creator of the world)? In 325 Constantine himself stepped in and summoned a synod of bishops to Nicaea (in what is now modern Turkey) to try to settle the crisis. Some of them argued that Jesus was a created being, separate and distinct from the eternal God who preceded creation; others believed that Jesus and God were of one and the same nature. In the end the latter group won out, and the council produced the Nicene Creed, a document that for the first time articulated a trinitarian concept of God and established a Christian orthodoxy of belief. At the edge of chaos, Nicaea had imposed order and uniformity.

It would not last for very long. In the centuries that followed, the capital of the Christian Church remained in Rome. But another major branch soon developed alongside it in the East (in places such as Greece, the Balkans, and Russia), with its own, separate center in Constantinople (today's Istanbul). The differences between the two traditions in theology, liturgy, rite, and church structure ultimately led to the Roman Catholicism and Orthodox Christianity of the present day. Yet in the West itself there was also a schism, a profound split in beliefs and practices and a transition from old forms to new ones. The Reformation, as the sixteenth century in Christian history is called, was the result of a wide range of factors and forces: corruption in the established church, indifference to and sometimes disdain for the encumbrances of religious rite and canon law, a new piety and theological awareness on the part of the laity, a growing sense of individualism in European culture, even the rise of nationalism and of the urban areas of Germany and Switzerland. The Reformation cast a spotlight not on the outer, collective ways that Christians expressed their faith, but on their inner, individual relationships with God. It was a movement that contributed to the birth pangs of the same modernity into which we ourselves were born.

The key figures during this bridge period were Martin Luther (1483–1546) and John Calvin (1509–1564). Luther, at the age of twenty-two, had originally intended to become a Catholic monk and had entered a monastery against the will of his father in 1505. It was his fear of death during a violent thunderstorm and his angst about not being able to stand in final judgment before God that first propelled him toward the priesthood, and it was this same overarching awareness of divine sovereignty that would inform his doctrine of "justification." As a monk Luther had observed mass, fasting, penitence, and penance with great fidelity, but none of these external acts seemed to solve for him the questions of his personal salvation. For Luther, faith alone is our path to heaven. Our "good works" and observance of the law are not the cause of our justification before God, but the result of it. It is divine grace, not human effort, that leads to the soul's final redemption. His new understanding of the church was a radical critique of what he viewed as a legalized church that had deviated from the message and spirit of the gospel.

One of the most legendary events in Luther's life, and the spark that many think ignited the Reformation, involved the dispute over indulgences, church documents issued by the pope that—for a fee—released a person from the punishments for sin. Pope Leo X had used indulgences as a fund-raising tool for the rebuilding of St. Peter's basilica in Rome, ordering an aggressive campaign for them in Germany. Luther viewed this approach to penance as the height of hypocrisy. He believed that the salvation of souls was the gift of God's grace—not something that could be bought with expensive indulgence certificates created to pay for elaborate edifices. The granting of forgiveness for sin belongs to the jurisdiction of God alone; the pope and his bishops have no authority in the matter.

Luther summed up his position in a set of ninety-five theses and sent them to the archbishop of Mainz as well as the academic public in 1517 (he had earned a doctorate in theology five years earlier). The document was disseminated everywhere. Luther became a polarizing figure, and the church quickly divided into opposing camps—those who supported Luther's reforms and vision for religious renewal and those who saw his ideas as heretical. His books were burned, he was investigated by Rome for heresy, and in 1521 he was officially excommunicated. Luther was a troubled person. He is almost as famous for his rabid anti-Semitism and intense misogyny as he is for his beliefs. But as a bridge figure, as a transitional force between old Christian religious expressions and new ones, his role in the rise of Protestantism in the West cannot be underestimated.

John Calvin, whose Swiss Reformation was in some ways based more on the ideals of the Renaissance than was Luther's, was another key bridge figure in Christian history. Calvinist ideas helped to inspire the Puritan revolution in England in 1645 as well as the initial colonization of our own country in the early seventeenth century. (Many aspects of Calvinism, such as the Puritan work ethic and the concept of election, or seeing ourselves as a "chosen nation," are with us still, even in secular America.) His was the second wave of the Protestant Reformation. His version of Christianity—and the far less aggressive and angry tactics he used to win over converts to it—was extremely appealing to the middle classes in the new and burgeoning European cities, whose residents, in the true spirit of the Renaissance, wanted to be liberated from what they felt was a repressive religious system.

Like Luther, Calvin believed in the absolute sovereignty of God, in the inability of men and women to contribute to their own salvation through deeds or rituals. Calvin urged a return to a simpler piety, founded on the gospel and free of the intermediaries—priests, bishops, saints—that had separated Christians from God in the medieval church. Protestantism rejected the Catholic hierarchy and the cult of the saints. It argued that only through a direct, personal relationship with God would a person discover his or her unique revelation and destiny. After Calvin's death in 1564, his followers began to direct this new faith more and more toward issues of predestination, hell, and damnation. The emphasis on eternal punishment for sin and severe self-scrutiny led the Puritans to treat their religious experience as an ordeal; God infused them not with joy or compassion, but with guilt. The struggle against Satan often led to despair or depression, but it also helped to inspire some of the Puritans to colonize the New World and brave the hardships they found on its soil.

The ancient Greek philosopher Heraclitus claimed that, like a river, life itself was in a constant state of flux, always shifting and changing, a bridge that ends only with death. Religion is no different. Though its various outer structures and paradigms have changed over the centuries (biblical and rabbinic, Catholic and Protestant), the same inner impulses that drove the earliest practitioners have also animated those who were active during transition periods. Spirituality, like life, is a dynamic process—it never stands still. Depending on our cultural backgrounds, age, and personal histories, our relationships with the organs of religion—its institutions, beliefs, rituals—ebb and flow. So do our relationships with God. Today, too, we are in a transition period, a bridge moment that will lead us into unknown territory. Religious life is changing before our eyes. We have no idea what new forms it will take as we enter this next century. Yet there is no other path but paralysis and death. Many of our spiritual traditions will survive the transition. Some probably will not. We need not be afraid: we must cross the bridge and aim for the other shore. It is not up to us to complete the task, as my tradition teaches us, but neither are we free to shy away from it.

conclusion

The primary goal of this book was to present some alternative paths to God, paths that can be at times uncomfortable and unexpected. I have not tried to argue that they are the only conduits to spirituality, or the best ones; each of us must find his or her own way. But I am convinced that the ideas and experiences I have written about are ones that have been neglected, to our detriment, by contemporary culture. Our encounters with the divine—and with our own souls—do not have to take place in the safe havens of churches or synagogues. They can occur in places that are unsettling, in places of agitation and, sometimes, even suffering. Yet the voices of our religious traditions seem to cry out to us: *Be strong and of good courage. God is as present in the darkness as in the light.*

This book is a call to widen, not narrow, the parameters of the spiritual life, to rattle our preconceptions about what constitutes "spirituality." I have tried to redress an imbalance in the way many people today talk about God and inner growth. God may be a crutch when we need comfort, but God can also be a thorn in our sides when we need (whether we know it or not) to be shaken and pushed. The Kotsker rebbe saw God in the flames and filth of our world. John of the Cross had a dark vision that led him to salvation. The Maggid of Mezeritch taught that at the highest spiritual levels, fear was not something to be avoided, but the very channel to mystical union.

I do fear one thing, though. Has this book merely been a rationalization of my personal experiences? Have I tried to justify, in spiritual terms, my own disposition and worldview? Is my disdain for the "warm and fuzzy" approach to spirituality simply the product of my own discomfort with—or aversion to—happiness and inner peace? For me, the last decade, and the road to my rabbinate, has not been easy. I have learned a great deal about myself and about my relationships with God and other people. I have also witnessed an imbalance in my own life, an inclination to favor raw experience over human interactions, dramatic epiphanies over subtle moments of insight. Up to now, that is where I have made my spiritual home. But it is a home that can often be cold and isolating.

I am easing away from the edge and searching for a center. I am trying to learn the wisdom of the middle way just as I have learned from the fringes. While I have few regrets about the different experiences I describe in this book, and while I am clearly not the first person to have found God outside of conventional religious contexts, I sense that the time has come for me to explore a new frontier: *community.* In the spring of 1999 I became the founding rabbi of a new congregation, The New Shul, in Greenwich Village, New York. As the spiritual leader of this young, creative, dynamic community—made up of artists, writers, musicians, and intellectuals—I have found the kind of fulfillment that was missing from my earlier adventures.

I do not have to give up my inner inclinations completely. As far as neighborhoods go, the Village has always had an "edge." But this edge has to do with people, not experiences. And most of the people who have joined our spiritual community have been estranged from the world of organized religion for a long time. How did we manage to attract them? Because of our philosophy: Create a community that stimulates and challenges the hearts, minds, and souls of its members, that is open to experimentation yet rooted firmly in the rites and rituals of our faith, that is caring without being coddling, and people will come. They have come.

Serving as a rabbi for a community of individuals is very different from the kind of rabbinate I have had up to now. I am beginning to hear the "still small voice" of God break through the thunder of Mount Sinai; I am beginning to see the sparks of divinity in the eyes of children and not only through the stars in the night sky. I am becoming *humanized.* But I know myself. I will always hear the call of the wild, the beckoning of fresh experiences and new frontiers. Yet I will have to come up with ways of incorporating that impulse into a spirituality that is centered in the here and now, in daily life, in relationships with other human beings. To paraphrase Frost, the edge is lovely, dark and deep, but I have promises to keep. And miles to go before I sleep. And miles to go before I sleep.

bibliographical sources

1 / *under lock and key*

Having an epiphany while behind bars is not as uncommon an experience as one might at first suspect. My challenge in this chapter was limiting myself to only two religious figures who seemed to have had it. Roman A. Foxbrunner wrote a very good but fairly academic book that explores the thought (but not much of the life) of Rabbi Shneur Zalman of Lyady called *Habad: The Hasidism of R. Shneur Zalman of Lyady* (Jason Aronson, Northvale, N.J., 1993). For a decent overview of the personal history of this great hasidic rebbe, look at the entry on him in the *Encyclopedia Judaica.* There are also many partisan, less disinterested books that have been written on Shneur Zalman that have been published by today's Habad community.

More material has been written on St. John of the Cross. Kieran Kavanaugh translated and compiled an excellent collection of his poetry and writings, *John of the Cross: Selected Writings* (New York, 1987), which was produced by the Paulist Press as one in a series of classic works of Western spirituality. For a beautiful translation of the mystic's most famous creation, read *Dark Night of the Soul: A Masterpiece in the Literature of Mysticism by St. John of the Cross,* translated and edited by E. Allison Peers (Image, New York, 1990). If you are interested solely in the monk's religious poetry, John Frederick Nims has put together *The Poems of St. John of the Cross,* a bilingual edition that contains the original Spanish texts and the accompanying English translations (University of Chicago Press, 1989).

2 / *strange fire*

The primary text that I used on demonology and the Inquisition was a book written by Paul Carus, *The History of the Devil and the Idea of Evil* (Open Court Publishing, Peru, Ill., 1994). Though it was written at the turn of the century and reflects the modernist, antireligion bias of its author, it is a very informative and colorful work that helps to capture just what happens to faith when it gets too close to the edge and gets consumed by its own excesses. I used several books for the Jewish section of this chapter. *The Maharal: The Mystical Philosophy of Rabbi Judah Loew of Prague* by Ben Zion Bokser (Jason Aronson, Northvale, N.J., 1994) and *Mystical Theology and Social Dissent: The Life and Works of Judah Loew of Prague* by Byron L. Sherwin (Associated University Presses, London, 1982) provide rich material on the life history of the Maharal, while *Golem: Jewish Magical and Mystical Traditions on the Artificial Anthropoid* by Moshe Idel (State University of New York Press, Albany, N.Y., 1990) and the final essay of *The Messianic Idea in Judaism*, "The Golem of Prague and the Golem of Rehovot," by Gershom Scholem (Schocken, New York, 1971), offer insightful analyses of the mystical and theological dimensions of the Golem. *Idolatry*, by Moshe Halbertal and Avishai Margalit (Harvard University Press, Cambridge, Mass., 1992), is a scholarly study on how the concept of idolatry has changed over the centuries.

3 / *forests of the night*

A great deal has been written on the psychology of fear, but surprisingly little about its relationship to Western spirituality. The way I have tried to explore the subject is by drawing out stories, parables, and theoretical writings from various religious books and articles. Much of the Christian material I use in this chapter comes from a book by Carol Lee Flinders, *Enduring Grace: Living Portraits of Seven Women Mystics* (HarperCollins, San Francisco, 1993). Although the book is about the personal histories and thought of these great women mystics, the theme of fear is common enough to the spiritual experiences of some of them that I found it immensely useful. Another book, a classic in the field (even though it is limited almost exclusively to Christian mystics), is Evelyn Underhill's *Mysticism* (Doubleday, New York, 1990). Her study provided me with additional interesting descriptions of some of the more frightening aspects of mystical union with God.

As far as Jewish sources go, *Essential Papers on Hasidism: Origins to Present*, edited by Gershon David Hundert (New York University Press, New York, 1991), offers an excellent overview of the hasidic period to which I refer throughout my own book. Martin Buber's collection of hasidic stories, *Tales of the Hasidim* (Schocken, New York, 1975), contains many interesting and famous mystical folktales, including the one about Rabbi Dov Baer's fateful and fearful meeting with the Baal Shem Tov that I mention in this chapter. Rivka Schatz Uffenheimer's *Hasidism as Mysticism: Quietistic Elements in Eighteenth Century Hasidic Thought* (Princeton University Press, Princeton, N.J., 1993) examines the phenomenon and role of fear in the theoretical writings of Dov Baer.

4 / *inward bound*

Though asceticism is not one of the most popular subjects in the Jewish tradition, it has been a personal favorite of mine for some time. *The Dead Sea Scrolls,* edited by G. Vermes (Penguin, New York, 1990), includes English translations of the most famous texts from the Qumran community in ancient Israel and offers fascinating insights into the spiritual culture and worldview of this extreme ascetic Jewish splinter group. "Ascetical Aspects of Ancient Judaism" by Steven D. Fraade explores Jewish asceticism during the time of antiquity. It can be found in *Jewish Spirituality from the Bible Through the Middle Ages,* an anthology of academic essays edited by Arthur Green (Crossroad, New York, 1988). Two books in particular were very helpful in my research on the Pietists of Medieval Germany: *The Book of the Pious,* translated, condensed, and annotated by Avraham Yaakov Finkel (Jason Aronson, Northvale, N.J., 1997), and the less partisan but more illuminating *Major Trends in Jewish Mysticism* by the great Israeli scholar Gershom Scholem (Schocken, New York, 1971).

While Christianity has a much more normative ascetic tradition, I had to limit myself to writing about a single "school"—the Desert Fathers—and a single individual—St. Catherine of Genoa. The best English collection I could find of the sayings of the desert hermits is in *Western Asceticism,* edited with a very good historical introduction by Owen Chadwick (Westminster Press, Philadelphia, 1958). Thomas Merton, the popular monk and author, published *The Wisdom of the Desert* (New Directions, New York, 1970), his own greatly abridged English translation of the sayings that affords the reader a more poetic, less analytical introduction to the material. I used Flinders's *Enduring Grace* and Underhill's *Mysticism* as the primary texts for examining the life and spiritual thought of St. Catherine. By drawing from the two books in combination, I felt that I gained a better picture of the mystic as a whole person, not just as a piece of intellectual history.

5 / on the silk road

The best biography on Rabbi Nachman of Bratslav that I am aware of is *Tormented Master: The Life and Spiritual Quest of Rabbi Nachman of Bratslav* by Arthur Green (Jewish Lights, Woodstock, Vt., 1992). Green describes, without any sentimentality about this hasidic rebbe who even today has disciples throughout the world, the many journeys and key ideas in Nachman's tortured life. Hundert's *Essential Papers on Hasidism* contains a few essays that discuss the nature and work of the itinerant maggid; "The Origins of Hasidism and Its Social and Messianic Foundations" by Benzion Dinur is the most informative. Jay P. Dolan's *The American Catholic Experience: A History from Colonial Times to the Present* (University of Notre Dame Press, South Bend, Ind., 1992) is filled with detailed information about the early Catholic (especially Jesuit) missionaries who journeyed to the New World with the hope of saving souls and experiencing rugged—but sometimes fatal—adventure. *A Religious History of the American People* by Sidney E. Ahlstrom (Yale University Press, New Haven, Conn., 1972) is another wonderful source of information on Christian missionary activity in America, particularly on those from the Protestant denominations.

6 / god undercover

I was certainly not the first person to see strong parallels between the writings of the Kotsker rebbe and Kierkegaard. *A Passion for Truth* by Abraham Joshua Heschel (Jewish Lights, Woodstock, Vt., 1995) remains the seminal book-length work to compare these two great nineteenth-century thinkers and mystics. *The Sayings of Menahem Mendel of Kotsk* by Simcha Raz (Jason Aronson, Northvale, N.J., 1995) offers a brief introduction to the Kotsker's life and a beautiful collection of some of his parables and aphorisms organized thematically. Unfortunately, as is the case with most of the hasidic masters, the majority of his material has not yet been translated into English.

A great deal has been written about Kierkegaard, and his major writings have been published in English. I used the translation of one of Kierkegaard's most "theological" books, *Philosophical Fragments* by Howard V. Hong and Edna H. Hong (Princeton University Press, Princeton, N.J., 1985), as a primary text and *Kierkegaard as Negative Theologian* by David R. Law (Oxford University Press, New York, 1993) and *Dialogical Philosophy from Kierkegaard to Buber* by Shmuel Hugo Bergman (State University of New York Press, Albany, N.Y., 1991) for a more academic analysis of his unique and influential thought. *The Prayers of Kierkegaard*, edited by Perry D. LeFevre (University of Chicago Press, 1963), chronicles the major events of the Danish thinker's life in the second part of the book, which contains ninety-nine of Kierkegaard's religious poems.

7 / *midnight sun*

The connection between nature and spirituality is a very ancient one, but I chose to focus on two of the more compelling religious personalities from the last three centuries (comparatively recent in historical terms). Jonathan Edwards was a major force in American religion and an important figure during the Great Awakening. *Jonathan Edwards: Basic Writings*, selected and edited by Ola Elizabeth Winslow (Meridian, New York, 1978), contains a short biography on his life and three essays that capture his views on the relationship between creation and the spiritual life: "Personal Narrative," excerpts from "The Images or Shadows of Divine Things," and "The Beauty of the World." Though not much is known about the life history of the Baal Shem Tov, we do have a number of (sometimes rather fantastic) stories about him and about his own views on nature. I drew from two books by Martin Buber, *Tales of the Hasidim* and *The Legend of the Baal-Shem* (Princeton University Press, Princeton, N.J., 1995).

8 / *views from the bridge*

Religions, like life itself, are in constant states of transition. I tried to write about just a few of the more monumental transitions in the Jewish and Christian traditions. *Ancient Israel: A Short History from Abraham to the*

Roman Destruction of the Temple, edited by Hershel Shanks (Biblical Archaeology Society, Washington, 1988), is an anthology of essays on eight significant and often tumultuous periods in the national and religious life of ancient Israel. While the essays were written mainly (but not exclusively) by academics, the book as a whole is very readable and is intended for the general reader. The Bible, of course, is itself an invaluable document for learning more about bridge moments in Jewish history.

Two books that were useful in examining religious paradigm shifts in Christianity were *A History of God: The 4000-Year Quest of Judaism, Christianity, and Islam* by the former nun Karen Armstrong (Alfred A. Knopf, New York, 1993) and *Great Christian Thinkers* by the theologian Hans Küng (Continuum, New York, 1997). While the personal biases of each author tend to come through their writing (Armstrong, for example, blasts Luther, while Küng praises his revolutionary ideas), each offers thoughtful theological insights into key Christian figures from Paul to Calvin. An essential source for reading the actual texts to which both of these books refer is *Documents of the Christian Church,* selected and edited by Henry Bettenson (Oxford University Press, New York, 1947).

about the author

Niles Elliot Goldstein is the founding rabbi of The New Shul in Greenwich Village, New York. He lectures widely on Jewish mysticism and spirituality and has taught at New York University and the Hebrew Union College–Jewish Institute of Religion. Goldstein was the voice behind "Ask the Rabbi" on the Microsoft Network and can now be reached at "Ask Rabbi Goldstein" at www.ifaith.com. He is the national Jewish chaplain for the Federal Law Enforcement Officers Association. His essays and poetry have appeared in *Newsweek* and many other publications, and he is the author or editor of four previous books, *Spiritual Manifestos: Visions for Renewed Religious Life in America from Young Spiritual Leaders of Many Faiths; Duties of the Soul: The Role of Commandments in Liberal Judaism; Judaism and Spiritual Ethics;* and *Forests of the Night: The Fear of God in Early Hasidic Thought.*

other bell tower books

Books that nourish the soul, illuminate the mind, and speak directly to the heart

Rob Baker
PLANNING MEMORIAL CELEBRATIONS
A Sourcebook
A one-stop handbook for a situation more and more of us are facing as we grow older.
0-609-80404-9 Softcover

Thomas Berry
THE GREAT WORK
Our Way into the Future
The grandfather of Deep Ecology teaches us how to move from a human-centered view of the world to one focused on the earth and all its inhabitants.
0-609-60525-9 Hardcover

Cynthia Bourgeault
LOVE IS STRONGER THAN DEATH
The Mystical Union of Two Souls
Both the story of the incandescent love between two hermits and a guidebook for those called to this path of soulwork.
0-609-60473-2 Hardcover

Madeline Bruser
THE ART OF PRACTICING
Making Music from the Heart
A classic work on how to practice music which combines meditative principles with information on body mechanics and medicine.
0-609-80177-5 Softcover

Marc David
NOURISHING WISDOM
A Mind/Body Approach to Nutrition and Well-Being
A book that advocates awareness in eating.
0-517-88129-2 Softcover

Joan Furman, MSN, RN, and David McNabb
THE DYING TIME
Practical Wisdom for the Dying and Their Caregivers
A comprehensive guide, filled with physical, emotional, and spiritual advice.
0-609-80003-5 Softcover

Bernard Glassman
BEARING WITNESS
A Zen Master's Lessons in Making Peace
How Glassman started the Zen Peacemaker Order and what each of us can do to make peace in our hearts and in the world.
0-609-60061-3 Hardcover; 0-609-80391-3 Softcover

Bernard Glassman and Rick Fields
INSTRUCTIONS TO THE COOK
A Zen Master's Lessons in Living a Life That Matters
A distillation of Zen wisdom that can be used equally well as a manual on business or spiritual practice, cooking or life.
0-517-88829-7 Softcover

Greg Johanson and Ron Kurtz
GRACE UNFOLDING
Psychotherapy in the Spirit of the Tao-te ching
The interaction of client and therapist illuminated through the gentle power and wisdom of Lao Tsu's ancient classic.
0-517-88130-6 Softcover

Selected by Marcia and Jack Kelly
ONE HUNDRED GRACES
Mealtime Blessings
A collection of graces from many traditions, inscribed in calligraphy reminiscent of the manuscripts of medieval Europe.
0-609-80093-0 Softcover

Jack and Marcia Kelly
SANCTUARIES
A Guide to Lodgings in Monasteries, Abbeys, and Retreats of the United States
For those in search of renewal and a little peace; described by *The New York Times* as "the *Michelin Guide* of the retreat set."
0-517-88517-4 Softcover

Marcia and Jack Kelly
THE WHOLE HEAVEN CATALOG
A Resource Guide to Products, Services, Arts, Crafts, and Festivals of Religious, Spiritual, and Cooperative Communities
All the things that monks and nuns do to support their habits!
0-609-80120-1 Softcover

Barbara Lachman
THE JOURNAL OF HILDEGARD OF BINGEN
A year in the life of the twelfth-century German saint—the diary she never had the time to write herself.
0-517-88390-2 Softcover

Stephen Levine
A YEAR TO LIVE
How to Live This Year as If It Were Your Last
Using the consciousness of our mortality to enter into a new and vibrant relationship with life.
0-609-80194-5 Softcover

Gunilla Norris

BEING HOME

A Book of Meditations

An exquisite modern book of hours, a celebration of mindfulness in everyday activities.

0-517-58159-0 Hardcover

Marcia Prager

THE PATH OF BLESSING

Experiencing the Energy and Abundance of the Divine

How to use the traditional Jewish practice of calling down a blessing on each action as a profound path of spiritual growth.

0-517-70363-7 Hardcover; 0-609-80393-X Softcover

Saki Santorelli

HEAL THY SELF

Lessons on Mindfulness in Medicine

An invitation to patients and health care professionals to bring mindfulness into the crucible of the healing relationship.

0-609-60385-X Hardcover; 0-609-80504-5 Softcover

Rabbi Rami M. Shapiro

MINYAN

Ten Principles for Living a Life of Integrity

A primer for those interested to know what Judaism has to offer the spiritually hungry.

0-609-80055-8 Softcover

Rabbi Rami M. Shapiro

WISDOM OF THE JEWISH SAGES

A Modern Reading of Pirke Avot

A third-century treasury of maxims on justice, integrity, and virtue—Judaism's principal ethical scripture.

0-517-79966-9 Hardcover

Jean Smith
THE BEGINNER'S GUIDE TO ZEN BUDDHISM
A comprehensive and easily accessible introduction that assumes no prior knowledge of Zen Buddhism.
0-609-80466-9 Softcover

Rabbi Joseph Telushkin
THE BOOK OF JEWISH VALUES
A Day-by-Day Guide to Ethical Living
Ancient and modern advice on how to remain honest in a morally complicated world.
0-609-60330-2 Hardcover

James Thornton
A FIELD GUIDE TO THE SOUL
A Down-to-Earth Handbook of Spiritual Practice
In the tradition of *The Seat of the Soul, The Soul's Code,* and *Care of the Soul,* a primer readers are calling "the Bible for the new millennium."
0-609-60368-X Hardcover; 0-609-80392-1 Softcover

Joan Tollifson
BARE-BONES MEDITATION
Waking Up from the Story of My Life
An unvarnished, exhilarating account of one woman's struggle to make sense of her life.
0-517-88792-4 Softcover

Michael Toms and Justine Willis Toms
TRUE WORK
Doing What You Love and Loving What You Do
Wisdom for the workplace from the husband-and-wife team of NPR's weekly radio program *New Dimensions.*
0-517-70587-7 Hardcover; 0-609-80212-7 Softcover

BUDDHA LAUGHING

A Tricycle *Book of Cartoons*

A marvelous opportunity for self-reflection for those who tend to take themselves too seriously.

0-609-80409-X Softcover

Ed. Richard Whelan

SELF-RELIANCE

The Wisdom of Ralph Waldo Emerson as Inspiration for Daily Living

A distillation of Emerson's spiritual writings for contemporary readers.

0-517-58512-X Softcover

Bell Tower books are for sale at your local bookstore or you may call Random House at 1-800-793-BOOK to order with a credit card.